EUROPE 1763-1970

HUGH GOUGH

LONGMAN

First published in 1974 by
THE EDUCATIONAL COMPANY OF IRELAND LIMITED,
incorporating
LONGMAN BROWNE AND NOLAN LIMITED,
Ballymount Road, Walkinstown, Dublin 12

This edition first published 1976 by Longman Group Limited, London.
Associated companies, branches and representatives throughout the world.

Cover design: John Skelton
Maps and diagrams: Robert Rogan

ISBN 0 582 22053 X

Printed in the Republic of Ireland by
Richview Press Limited, Dublin

Contents

Acknowledgments

The publishers wish to thank the following for permission to reproduce illustrations in this book:
National Library of Ireland; National Museum of Ireland; British Museum; National Portrait Gallery; National Maritime Museum; Science Museum; Imperial War Museum; Victoria and Albert Museum; Museum of English Rural Life, University of Reading; Wellington Museum; London Museum; Wellcome Trust; Sir John Soane's Museum; Marylebone Cricket Club; National Film Archive; National Gallery; Parker Gallery; Wilberforce House; Institute of Agricultural Economics, University of Oxford; Liverpool City Libraries; City of Liverpool Museums; Walker Art Gallery; Bedfordshire County Record Office; Leicester Museums and Art Gallery; Halifax Museum; National Gallery of Scotland; Marconi Company Limited; Radio Times Hulton Picture Library; Popperfoto; Camera Press; Keystone Press Agency; Associated Press; Documentation Française; Bulloz; Giraudon; Musée du Louvre; Bibliothèque Nationale; Musée Carnavalet; Musée National du Chateau de Versailles; Musée de la Légion d'Honneur; Musée Bernadotte; Archives Nationale; Collection Prince Murat; Collection de Castellane; Institut Pasteur; Musées de Rouen; Staatsbibliothek Berlin; Staatliche Kunstsammlungen Dresden; Deutsches Museum München; Historisches Museum Frankfurt am Main; Ullstein Bilderdienst; Österreichische Nationalbibliothek; Krupp, Essen; Museo del Prado; United Nations Organisation; Yale University Art Gallery; Museum of Modern Art, New York; Library of Congress, U.S.A.

Introduction

The history of Europe over the last two hundred years is packed with excitement and interest, for so many of the achievements and problems that it contains are now part of our everyday life. In this book I have tried to provide a clear, useful account of European history for the CSE candidate who finds difficulty in coping with the more detailed textbooks available at this level.

Inevitably in this space and for this level the content is not comprehensive. I have dealt here with some of the major events and themes of the period: the political revolutions, the creation of nation states and the two world wars. But mainly I have concentrated on social history, for the dramatic changes that have taken place here are perhaps the most significant developments of recent times. Diplomatic history is omitted, as is the history of ideas, much political history and some major events (the Spanish Civil War, for example) I felt to be too complex for treatment at this level.

As well as being selective in treatment, I have tried to write in simple and concrete terms. Broad themes are illustrated where possible with specific examples, and the events are told through the lives of people involved in them. There are over 400 illustrations which, with their captions, are integral to the content.

The aim has been to ensure that readers gain a basic understanding of the main developments and become interested in them. They will then have a basis for further, more detailed, work.

Hugh Gough

A medallion of a slave in chains. This was made by the potter Josiah Wedgwood, who supported Wilberforce's campaign, and it became the official seal of the Slave Emancipation Society.

1 Change Comes to Europe, 1760–89

During the eighteenth century the people of Europe began to notice that their way of life was changing. They were becoming more prosperous and more healthy. They read books and picked up new ideas. Soon they started to talk about the rights of man, and to argue about the way in which they were governed.

In this chapter you will read about all these changes. You will also see the effect that they had on the people of Europe.

Before the coming of the railways the Elephant and Castle Inn was one of the most popular coaching inns for travellers on their way south out of London. You can see it on the left of this picture, with the church next door.

1 The Growth of Trade

The eighteenth century was an age of great prosperity for the merchants and traders of Europe. Trade was good and their profits were high. Every week of the year the large sea ports were crammed full of sailing ships loaded with cargoes from distant lands.

As soon as the ships came into port, dockers worked hard to unload them. They heaved the cargoes off the ships and onto large horse-drawn carts. These carts were bound for the cities and towns that lay further inland. Once they were fully loaded they set off along the rough and muddy roads. The horses lumbered forward and the carts creaked under the heavy load. The journey was usually very slow. Most carts could only cover about twenty miles in a day. Often a wheel broke or the cart stuck fast in the mud. Sometimes the driver was drunk, so that the cart ended up in a ditch! These accidents only made the journey slower still. However, when the cart eventually arrived at its destination, the goods that it carried were quickly unloaded. They were then put up for sale in local shops or in the market place.

Europe Trades with the World

What sort of goods came to the towns and villages of Europe in this way? There were many different sorts. There was silk from China, cotton from India, and brightly-coloured dyes from the tiny islands of the Far East. There was gold and silver from the rich mines of South America. There were furs

Sailing ships arriving in Europe with cargoes from distant lands.

Customers chatting to a waitress in a coffee-house.

and timber from Canada, and many strange sorts of fish. There was also coffee, sugar and tobacco from the sunny islands of the Caribbean.

All these goods were extremely popular—especially coffee and tobacco. Most towns in Europe had their coffee-houses where people could sit in comfort drinking coffee and smoking a pipe. The coffee-house was a place where people could read the newspapers or gossip about local affairs. It was a pleasant place to spend the day.

The merchants and traders of Europe did good business throughout the

Inside the illustration:

A. La façon de faire marcher les bœufs qui font tourner le moulin
B. Le grand Rouleau de la machine
C. Les petits Rouleaux qui brisent les cannes
D. Le Tuyau par ou le suc découle
E. Le Bassin qui reçoit le suc
F. Les deux vaisseaux remplis d'eau ou de que autre liqueur qui dégoute sur les essieux, afin d'empecher l'embrazement que le mouvement assidu pourroit causer

La Figure des Moulins a Sucre

G. L'essieu du grand Rouleau qui fait mouvoir toutes les roues de la machine
H. Les pieces de bois entrelassées qui lient et serrent la machine
I. Les planches sur lesquelles les Negres posent les cannes de Sucre
K. Les grandes chaudieres dans lesquelles on fait bouillir le suc jusques à ce qu'il soit épais
L. Les Negres qui servent le Moulin, et qui poussent les Cannes entre les Rouleaux.

Slaves working on a sugar plantation in the Caribbean.

eighteenth century. People were becoming more wealthy. They wanted more and more of the goods that came from far-off lands.

Trade with the Caribbean

The biggest trade of all was with the islands of the Caribbean, which produced coffee, sugar and tobacco. These products were grown on huge farms known as 'plantations'. Work on the plantations was extremely hard. People died from disease and overwork. So, to replace them, the plantation owners bought negroes from West Africa. These were shipped across the Atlantic to the Caribbean and made to work as slaves on the plantations.

The Slave Trade

The business of supplying these slaves was done by merchants and traders from Europe. They were known as 'slave traders'. They sent their ships to the coast of West Africa, loaded up with guns, mirrors, jewels and brightly-coloured clothes. They then gave these to the local tribal chiefs in exchange

for slaves. The slaves were then loaded on board ship, put below deck and chained together. The ship then set sail for the Caribbean.

The voyage to the Caribbean took several weeks. It was often very dangerous. One ship, the *Laughing Sally*, hit a whale in mid-Atlantic and sank. All her crew and her slaves were drowned, but the whale survived! On other ships disease often broke out among the slaves. Sometimes most of the slaves died and their bodies had to be thrown overboard.

When the ships reached the Caribbean, it was time to do business. The slaves were all washed, perfumed, and put up for sale to the plantation owners. They usually fetched a good price. With the money that they made from the sale the merchants bought sugar, coffee and tobacco from the plantation owners. They then shipped this back to Europe and sold it.

This model of the interior of a slave ship shows how closely packed together slaves were for their trip across the Atlantic. Each slave had a small space to lie down in, about five feet by two; he was taken out for exercise once a day and fed twice. No wonder so many of them died on board ship.

A slave ship being attacked and captured.

5

William Wilberforce (1759-1833). He was one of the few people who spoke out in Britain against the slave trade. In 1807 he persuaded Parliament to pass a law banning British merchants from taking any further part in it. In most other European countries the slave trade was banned by 1820.

Opposite
The growth of Liverpool in the eighteenth century.

The Cruelty of Slavery

As you can see, the slave trade was extremely cruel. Between 1600 and 1800 over seven million negroes from Africa were sold as slaves in the islands of the Caribbean. They were separated from their families and their homes. They lost their freedom and their self-respect. They usually died at a young age because of overwork.

Nevertheless, merchants made such great profits from the slave trade that few people ever dared to speak out against it. Many towns and cities became prosperous from the trade. In London and Bristol all the richest merchants were 'slavers'. They built fine houses and wide streets with the money that they made. They also gave employment to hundreds of people. Liverpool owed all its wealth to the slave trade. In 1700 it was only a small village. By 1800 it was a large and prosperous city, thanks to the wealth of the slavers. In France also there were many ports which were full of prosperous slave traders. The most famous of these ports was Bordeaux.

A Wealthy Slaver

Let us take a look at one of the slave traders of Bordeaux: François Bonnaffé. François was born in 1723. His parents were not very rich, so he had to leave school at an early age. He went to work as an office boy in a trading company. The hours of work were long. The work was boring. François became very unhappy.

Soon he began to notice that many merchants were making a good deal of money from the slave trade. So he took a risk. He invested some of his hard-earned savings in a slaving voyage. The voyage was a success and François earned enough money to give up his job as an office boy. He started up his own business and soon became the most famous and wealthy merchant in Bordeaux. He was always a very vain man. His clothes were made of velvet and silk, and he wore a well powdered wig. Whenever he went to the docks to inspect a cargo he wore white gloves so that his hands would not get dirty. When he died in 1791 he left a huge fortune to his son: six million pounds in money, two ships, twenty-three houses and hundreds of acres of land. The poor office boy had become a millionaire!

Many other merchants became rich like François Bonnaffé. They made their fortune and became famous. People bowed to them as they passed by in the street. However, many merchants wanted to do more than just become famous. They began to demand a say in the government of their country. In the next section we shall see how many writers in the eighteenth century supported their demands.

6

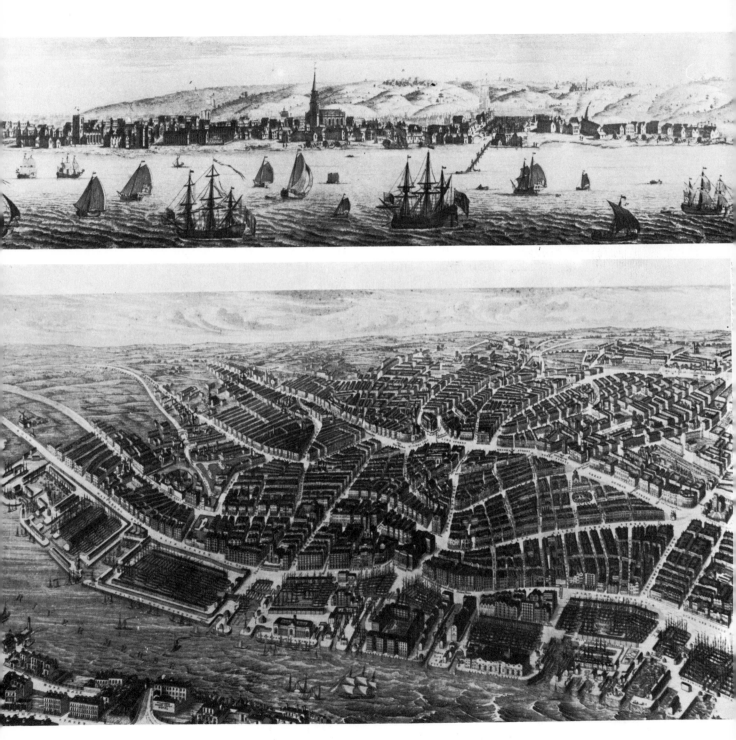

Sir Isaac Newton.

2 The Enlightenment

The eighteenth century was not only an age of wealth and prosperity. It was also an age of new ideas and great discoveries. People at the time said that these new ideas threw new light onto old problems. So they called their age the age of the 'Enlightenment'. The name has stuck ever since.

Let us take a look at some of the leading thinkers of the Enlightenment, so that we can see what their new ideas were.

Sir Isaac Newton

One of the most important thinkers was an English scientist, Sir Isaac Newton (1642–1727). Newton was the son of a farmer, and was educated at the University of Cambridge. It was there that he became interested in mathematics and astronomy. In 1687, after many years of hard work, he published an important book, *The Mathematical Principles of Natural Philosophy*. In this he showed that the universe was like a well-oiled automatic machine. The way in which the sun, moon and stars moved around the sky could all be explained by three simple laws: the laws of gravity. Newton explained what gravity did and showed how people could understand it with the help of some simple mathematics.

It was an astonishing discovery. Man could now understand the complicated workings of the universe. One poet put it this way:

> Nature and Nature's laws
> Lay hid in Night.
> God said, 'Let Newton be!'
> And there was light.

John Locke.

John Locke

John Locke (1632–1704) was also an Englishman, but was more interested in human beings than in the sun and stars. He was born in the county of Somerset, and was educated at the University of Oxford. For much of his life he was interested in politics, and was once exiled from England because of his political opinions. He was mainly interested in improving the way in which people behaved and in changing the way that they were governed. In one of his books, *An Essay Concerning Human Understanding*, he said that the way that people behaved depended on the way that they had been educated. As a result of this people began to take a greater interest in education. In another book, *Treatise on Civil Government*, Locke suggested how governments could be improved. He said that governments should obey the wishes of the people, and look after their interests. Therefore, he wanted parliaments to be more powerful, so that they could keep a close watch on the action of kings. He suggested that parliaments should have the power to vote laws and that kings should see that those laws were carried out. In this way, he argued, neither parliament nor king would be too powerful. Each would work in harmony with the other.

Locke's writings were read by many people and translated into many languages.

Montesquieu

One of the people who read Locke's books was a French nobleman, baron de Montesquieu (1689–1755). He lived in a big draughty castle near the town of Bordeaux in western France. Even when he was a child he read many books, and the study where he did most of his reading can still be seen today. He also travelled widely. He visited England and Italy, where he met many of the leading thinkers of his day. He talked with them late into the night. Many people thought that he was a boring person, and everyone certainly agreed that his wife was very ugly indeed. However, they had to admit that he had interesting ideas. His most famous book was called *The Spirit of the Laws*, published in 1748. In this he agreed with Locke that the powers of the king should be kept in check by a parliament. Thus, people could remain free and still have a say in the running of their own country. We shall see later how these views were put into effect in America.

Montesquieu.

Voltaire

Voltaire (1694–1788) was a very different sort of man from Montesquieu. He was the son of a Parisian lawyer. However, he spent most of his life away from France because his opinions annoyed the French Government. Voltaire was a witty and clever person who was very entertaining to talk to. However, he also enjoyed arguing, and this often got him into trouble. During his long lifetime he wrote thousands of letters, and many pamphlets, poems and books. In these he put forward his main views. He attacked the powers of the Catholic Church, and argued in favour of religious toleration. He also wanted governments to be reformed to give more power to the people. He was a great admirer of the English Parliament.

Diderot.

Denis Diderot

Denis Diderot (1713–84) lived at the same time as Voltaire, but the two men rarely met. Diderot was one of a family of thirteen children, and his father was a humble knifemaker from a small town in the east of France. At first Diderot studied for the priesthood, but soon changed his mind. He became a writer instead. He was always very poor, and spent much of his time in a small dark room in Paris writing pamphlets and books. His most famous

Voltaire had a reputation for hard work. This picture shows him dictating a letter to his secretary as he begins to get dressed in the morning.

Opposite
A page from Diderot's *Encyclopedia,* showing many of the different ways of farming in France during the eighteenth century.

work was a huge *Encyclopedia* of thirty-three volumes, which took him over twenty years to finish. It was published from 1751 to 1772. Diderot wrote many of the articles himself and his friends wrote the others. The *Encyclopedia* was meant to be a description of all the things that existed in the world—

11

much like any other encyclopedia. However, it also had many articles in it which criticised the Church and the government. Because of this Diderot often found himself in trouble. Nevertheless, the *Encyclopedia* was one of the most famous books of the age, and was read by many people. It made people think about the need for changes in their government and their way of life.

Jean-Jacques Rousseau

If Diderot was poor, so too was Jean-Jacques Rousseau (1712–78). Rousseau was born in Geneva, but was abandoned by his parents while he was only a child. At first he tried his hand at many jobs, and even composed an opera. Yet, it was as a writer that he became famous. He was always a lonely person and made things worse by quarrelling with most of his friends. In his books he called for people to return to the simple life, away from the crowded cities. He thought that the best form of government was a democracy, where people could govern themselves. He also believed, like Locke, that people would improve if they were given better education. Although he died poor, Rousseau's ideas have lived on into our own century. Nowadays many people who are interested in government and education still read the works of Rousseau.

An example of eighteenth-century architecture: the huge town square in Dresden in the eighteenth century. The massive church in the background, which towers over all the other buildings, was built during the early eighteenth century; it was totally destroyed by an air-raid in 1945, at the end of the Second World War.

Some of the Ideas of the Enlightenment

All these different writers with their new ideas may seem rather confusing to you. But if you look back over this section, you will see that most of the writers agreed on certain basic principles. Some of them believed that education was important. Others thought that the Church was too powerful. All of them wanted changes to be made in government. They wanted people to be able to have a greater say in their own affairs.

Now, we saw in the last section that merchants and traders also wanted a greater say in the running of their country. So they read the books written by men such as Locke and Voltaire. They agreed with their ideas. But they did not know how to obtain the reform in government that they wanted. In the next section we shall see that events in America provided them with the answer to this problem.

3   The American War of Independence

The American War of Independence was one of the most important events in the history of the world. It took place between 1775 and 1783. In it the people who lived in the British colonies of North America won their independence from Britain. They then established the United States of America as a free and independent country.

What effect did this have in Europe? To find out the answer to this question we must first see how the 'colonists' won their independence.

The British Colonies in America

In the mid-eighteenth century there were thirteen colonies in North America. They were all on the east coast. Few people knew what lay further inland, and even fewer had the courage to find out. They were afraid of being attacked by Red Indians or wild beasts.

All the colonists had gone to America from Europe in search of a better life. Many of them had left Europe in order to avoid persecution for their religious views. Others had gone in search of fame and fortune. Most of them were English, but there were also people from Scotland, Ireland, Holland and elsewhere.

All the colonists were governed by the king and parliament in London. The colonists had always been quite happy with this arrangement. Most of them thought of themselves as being British rather than American. They did not wish to become a separate country.

However, in many ways they were very different from the people who lived in Britain. Most of them were the sons and daughters of people who

Rousseau.

Original thirteen colonies of Britain in North America.

CANADA

NEW HAMPSHIRE
MASSACHUSETTS
NEW YORK
RHODE ISLAND
CONNECTICUT
NEW JERSEY
PENNSYLVANIA
DELAWARE
MARYLAND
VIRGINIA
NORTH CAROLINA
SOUTH CAROLINA
GEORGIA

OCEAN

ATLANTIC

GULF OF MEXICO

American patriot Samuel Adams (1722-1803). He was one of those who signed the Declaration of Independence.

had emigrated. They had been brought up in America and had never seen Britain at all. Many colonists also spoke with a strange American accent. British people laughed at this and thought it most peculiar. The colonists were also proud of the fact that they were more free than people in Britain. There no noblemen in America. No one had special privileges. Everyone had equal rights. So, although they did not realise it, the colonists were gradually becoming more American than British.

14

The Rumblings of War

It was not long before the colonists did, in fact, begin to realise this. It all started with an argument over money. Between 1756 and 1763 the British fought a war with France for the territory of Canada. They won the war and forced the French to leave Canada for good. This protected the American colonies from the danger of a French invasion. Therefore, the British government decided that the colonists should help to pay for some of the costs of the war. Between 1763 and 1773 they introduced new taxes into the colonies: taxes on such things as sugar, tea, newspapers and books.

The colonists objected very strongly to this. They claimed that the new taxes were illegal, because the British parliament contained no elected representative from the colonies. How could they be expected to pay taxes that they had not even voted for? Certainly they did not intend to pay them, and they used the slogan: 'No taxation without representation'. Men such as Samuel Adams, John Hancock and Thomas Jefferson, led this resistance. A group of people who called themselves the Sons of Liberty helped them by organising huge demonstrations. Many colonists refused to buy British goods and government officials refused to collect the new taxes.

The Boston Tea Party

The whole question came to a head in 1773. In that year, the British government allowed a large trading company, the East India Company, to sell ten million pounds of its tea in the colonies at a very low price. The colonists were furious. So far they had avoided paying the tax on tea by smuggling it into the country. Now, they would be forced to buy British tea. This meant that they would have to pay the tax. Secretly, a group of them decided to take action to prevent this.

In late 1773, the first tea ship, the *Dartmouth*, sailed into Boston harbour. On the night of 16 December, soon after the ship had docked, a gang of men crept aboard, disguised as Mohawk Indians. Quickly and quietly they dumped all the tea overboard into the muddy waters of the harbour. This Boston Tea Party soon became famous throughout the colonies. It showed how strongly the colonists opposed British policies.

The British quickly took action to prevent any further trouble. Yet, this only made the colonists more determined. Soon it became obvious that war would break out. On 19 April 1775 a small force of British troops was sent to the town of Concorde to seize guns that were being stored there by some colonists. On the way they were ambushed in the small village of Lexington. Many British troops were killed, and those who survived had to struggle back to their base. The war had begun.

Another American patriot, John Hancock (1737–93). He was the first to sign the Declaration of Independence.

Thomas Jefferson (1743-1826). A strong supporter of American independence, he was chairman of the committee that drew up the Declaration of Independence in 1776. He went on to become President of the U.S.A. from 1801-9.

15

Just over a year later, on 4 July 1776, the Americans issued their Declaration of Independence. This gave the reasons for their quarrel with Britain, and declared the independence of the new United States of America. The Fourth of July is still celebrated as a public holiday in the United States.

The War of Independence
Although they had declared their independence, the Americans still had to win the war. At first everyone thought that they would lose. The British had a well-trained army already on the spot. Their navy was also able to bring in large supplies of extra men and equipment. Nevertheless, the British wasted their advantages, and this gave the Americans the chance to organise their

According to the Stamp Act of 1764, stamps were to be placed on all newspapers, broadsides, pamphlets, licences, leases or other legal documents. On the day it came into effect stamps were burned in the streets of Boston, bells tolled, shops closed, flags hung at half mast and newspapers printed deathsheads where the stamps were to have been placed.

16

The Boston Tea Party, with the crates of tea slowly sinking in the water.

George Washington (1732-99) was a wealthy farmer from the state of Virginia. His father had died when he was only eleven years old and he had been brought up by his brother. He first fought as a soldier against the French in Canada, and later against the Indians. He was a proud man, rather snobbish and with no sense of humour. When he was elected President he made it a rule that all people should stand up when he came into a room and remain standing until he had left. One of his colleagues once said: 'I fear we may have exchanged George the Third for George the First'.

forces. George Washington, commander-in-chief of the American army, improved the discipline of his men, and made sure that they were well armed. Soon the Americans were able to hold their own against the British on land. At sea their position became better in 1778 when the French joined the war against Britain. French ships broke the British command of the sea, and people began to realise that the Americans could win the war. In October 1781 the main British army, led by General Cornwallis, finally surrendered to Washington's army at Yorktown. The war was over. Two years later the

British signed the Treaty of Versailles, which established the independence of the United States of America. A new nation was born.

The Constitution of the United States

The Americans were still left with the problem of setting up a constitution for their new country. This was not an easy thing to do, because some of the individual colonies did not want to lose any of their powers to a central government. The problem was solved by a special meeting of representatives of all thirteen colonies in Philadelphia in 1787. Each of the colonies (now called states) was allowed to keep control of their own local affairs. However, a central government was set up to deal with matters which involved all states, such as foreign affairs, justice, and war. This central government was made up of:

a President elected by the people, with the power to run the government;
a Senate and a House of Representatives elected by the people, with the power to vote laws and taxes.

This new constitution was put into effect in 1789, and George Washington was elected as the first President of the United States of America.

That, briefly, is the story of how the United States of America was established. But why was all this so important for the people of Europe? Simply because the Americans put into practice many of the ideas of the Enlighten-

19

The port of Philadelphia.

Opposite
The American Declaration of Independence of 1776 with the pictures of some of its leading signatories at the top and the symbols of each of the thirteen states around the edge.

ment thinkers. They fought for the right to control their own affairs. They then set up a government to carry out their wishes.

To see what this really meant, let us take another look at the Declaration of Independence of 1776. Here are the opening words of it:

> We hold these truths to be self-evident, that all men are created equal, that they are endowed by their Creator with certain unalienable rights, that among these are life, liberty, and the pursuit of happiness. That to secure these rights, Governments are instituted among men, deriving their just powers from the consent of the governed.

In simple words, this meant that all people should have equal rights, including the right to have a say in the government of their country. This was what the Enlightenment thinkers had said. The Americans had put it into practice. Now it was up to the people in Europe to follow their example.

20

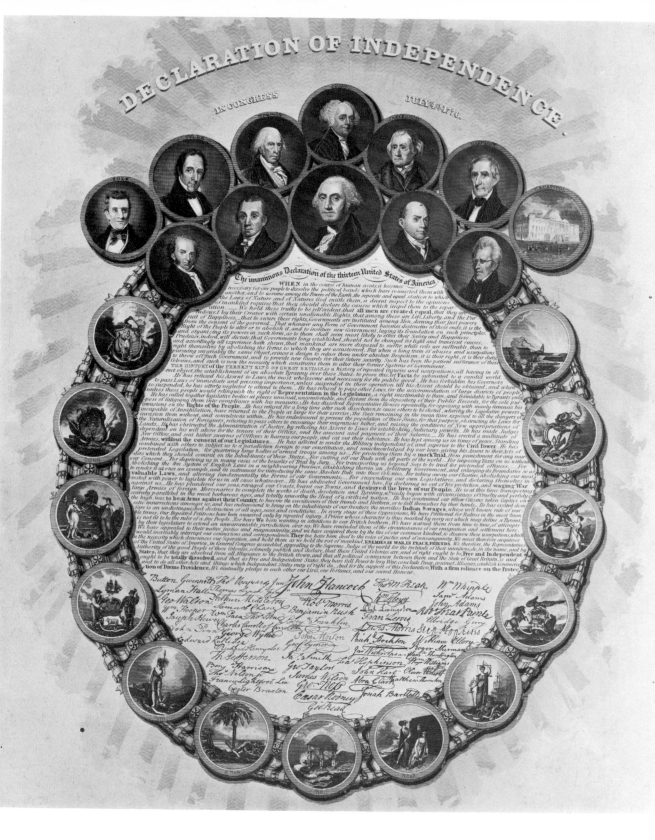

TO DO

1 You are a cabin boy on a slaving voyage, setting sail from Liverpool. Write a diary about the adventures of your voyage to Africa, the Caribbean Islands, and back again. Don't forget to write about the captain of your ship, the slaves and the plantation owners.
2 Find out more about William Wilberforce and his campaign to abolish the slave trade.
3 You are a newspaper reporter and you have an interview with Voltaire. Tell your readers what sort of a person he is and what sort of ideas he has. Do the same for other thinkers of the Enlightenment.
4 Write a short account of the life of George Washington. If you can, use an encyclopedia to help you find out more about him.
5 Look at a modern map of the United States. Whereabouts are the original thirteen colonies?
6 Take up your textbook on Irish History for this period. Read about the effect that the American War of Independence had on Ireland.

TO READ

The Eighteenth Century 1718–83, J. S. Milward and H. P. Arnold-Craft, Hutchinson.
John Newton and the Slave Trade, Then and There Series, Bernard Martin, Longman Group.
The American Revolution 1775–83, Then and There Series, Clorinda Clarke, Longman Group.
The Young American Revolution, Then and There Series, Clorinda Clarke, Longman Group.
The Slave Trade and its Abolition, Jackdaw Series no. 12, Jackdaw Publications.
The American Revolution, Jackdaw Series no. 14, Jackdaw Publications.

DATELINE

1687 Newton publishes *Mathematical Principles of Natural Philosophy.*
1748 Montesquieu publishes *Spirit of the Law.*
1751 Diderot begins work on his *Encyclopedia.*
1762 Rousseau publishes *The Social Contract.*
1773 The Boston Tea Party.
1775 Beginning of the American War of Independence.
1776 American Declaration of Independence.
1783 The Treaty of Versailles: Independence for the United States of America.

2 The French Revolution, 1789–99

1789 is one of the most famous dates in the history of the world. It was the year in which the French Revolution began. The French Revolution did not only change the way of life for people in France. It also affected the lives of people in other parts of Europe. Neither France nor Europe would ever be the same again.

In this chapter you will find out why the Revolution happened. You will also read about famous events such as the fall of the Bastille, the execution of the French King, and the long Reign of Terror.

Wealthy people strolling round the gardens of the Palais Royal in the centre of Paris just before the revolution. Behind them, underneath the windows, are some of the shops and stalls that sold clothes and jewellery.

1 The Causes of the Revolution

In 1789 France was the strongest country in Europe. She had large armies, a good navy, and a growing population. Her kings were admired everywhere because of their majesty and dignity. Her writers, such as Voltaire and Diderot, wrote books that were read everywhere because of their new ideas.

The Court at Versailles

Many tourists made the journey to France to see the royal court at the palace

The royal palace at Versailles being built during the reign of Louis XIV (1661-1714).

of Versailles, some twelve miles outside Paris. There they saw the huge buildings and the magnificent gardens, all built during the reign of Louis XIV. They marvelled at the hundreds of courtiers who swarmed through the wide corridors, and listened for the buzz of excitement as the king approached. Many of the most powerful noblemen in France lived at the Court of Versailles, and worked in the service of the king. Versailles was truly the house of the King of France, and the centre of the French government.

Why was this splendour destroyed by the revolution in 1789? To answer that question we shall have to go back a little in time. For part of the answer can be found in the character of the king, and part of it in the problems of the French people.

Louis XVI and Marie-Antoinette

Louis XVI became King of France in 1774. Most people who knew him said that he was a kind and simple person, who always tried to do what he thought was right. However, he did not like making decisions, and often changed his mind about his policies. This made it difficult for his ministers to get things done. Most of the time the king was bored with affairs of state, and preferred to go hunting, or to work at his favourite hobby of making watches. Good watch makers do not make good kings.

The queen, Marie-Antoinette, was an Austrian princess. She had married Louis XVI in 1770, and came to live with him in Versailles. She was pretty but proud, and had a great deal of influence over the king. Unfortunately she knew very little about France, or about the problems of the French people. This made her oppose any change in government, and also made her very unpopular with ordinary people.

The Problem of the Royal Debt

Louis XVI and Marie-Antoinette were certainly not the best people to govern France, particularly as the country was faced with serious problems. The most urgent problem was that of money. Ever since the reign of Louis XIV the French government had been in debt. Every year it spent more money than it received in taxes. Every year ministers were forced to borrow money from bankers in order to pay the costs of government. By 1787 the government owed so much money that the bankers were reluctant to lend more. Soon the government would be bankrupt. Something had to be done.

The Nobility and Clergy resist Reforms

The king and his ministers decided that the only answer was to increase

A portrait of Louis XVI, King of France from 1774–92. This portrait was drawn in 1792, during the revolution, when the King was in prison; note the stern look, but also the sadness in his eyes.

Marie-Antoinette (1755–93). She never understood the problems of poor people and it is said that, in 1789, when she was told that crowds in Paris were rioting because of a shortage of bread, she replied 'Let them eat cake then!'.

A cartoon showing the 'third estate' carrying the burden of the nobility and the clergy who did not pay taxes. The caption underneath read: 'Let's hope that this game will all be over soon'.

taxation. This, they thought, would give the government more money so that they could pay off their debts. However, this brought up a serious problem. The richest people in the country—the nobility and the clergy—did not pay taxes. Ever since medieval times they had been excused from paying them. This was because they served their country in other ways: the nobility fought for their country and the clergy prayed for it. This left the task of paying taxes to the rest of the country: the merchants, traders, lawyers, peasants and workers. They were called the 'third estate'.

By the eighteenth century many people in France thought that this system was unfair. They pointed out that the nobility were extremely rich. They owned one-fifth of all the land in France. Many of the clergy were also very rich, particularly the bishops and abbots. Was it fair, they asked, that such rich people should not have to pay taxes? Surely the nobility and clergy could help to pay off the government's debts?

The king's ministers certainly thought that they could. So, in 1787 and 1788 they tried to persuade the nobility and clergy to pay the same taxes as everybody else. The nobility and clergy refused. They still claimed that they were special people, with different rights from the ordinary people. They had no wish to pay taxes, and claimed that the government had no right to force them to. Instead they said that the government should call an Estates General—a kind of national parliament, which would decide what to do. The king had little option but to agree. In July 1788 he issued a proclamation, ordering elections to be held for an Estates General. It was to meet in May 1789.

The Complaints of the Third Estate

The nobility and clergy were well satisfied with this. They had prevented the government from making them pay taxes. Now they looked forward to the Estates General, for they hoped to dominate its debates and discussions.

The Estates General consisted of three houses (they were often called 'estates'). One was elected by the clergy. Another was elected by the nobility. The third was elected by the third estate. Each house met in its own separate chamber, and its decision counted as one vote. As a result, the nobility and the clergy could always out-vote the third estate by two votes to one. This meant that they could stop any attempt to reform France or to abolish their own privileges.

When the elections for the Estates General were held, many members of the third estate complained about this system of voting. They said that everyone in the country should be treated equally. They wanted all the people elected to the Estates General to sit in one room and vote as equals.

La Fayette and the Abbé Sieyès

One person who argued for this sort of change was a young army general called La Fayette. He had fought for the Americans in their War of Independence against Britain. In America he saw that all men were treated as equals and that everyone had a say in government. He wanted this to be done in France.

Another supporter of the third estate was the Abbé Sieyès. He was a quiet, thoughtful person, who had been forced to go into the Church against his own will. Unlike La Fayette, he fought with the pen, not the sword. He published a pamphlet called *What is the Third Estate?* In this he claimed that the members of the third estate were the most hard-working people in the country. Because of this, he said, they should be treated as the equals of the nobles and clergy.

Many people agreed with Sieyès. As a result, people who held these views were elected by the third estate as deputies to the Estates General. They took with them lists of the changes that they wanted to see in France. These lists, called 'grievance lists', were drawn up by the people who elected them. They included demands for equal rights, elected parliaments, and a more fair system of taxation.

The Revolt of the Poor

Most of these ideas were supported by the poor. We saw earlier that the merchants and traders of France grew rich during the eighteenth century. However, at the same time, the peasants and workers grew steadily poorer. As the population of France grew, land got scarce and jobs became scarcer still. Prices rose much faster than wages, and by 1789 many people were worse off then ever before.

To make things even worse there was a terrible harvest in 1788. Bad weather ruined the crops and food soon became scarce. Prices rose quickly and many workers lost their jobs. Bands of beggars roamed the countryside in search of food. Thousands went to the woods and lived on berries, bark and roots. Others begged in the streets of towns. Some just died from lack of food.

These poor and starving people badly needed help. They believed that changes should be made in government so that such bad times would never happen again. So they supported the deputies of the third estate in the Estates General. They wanted the privileges of the nobility and the clergy to be abolished. They wanted a new France and a better chance in life. In the next section we shall see how the events of 1789 brought about this better chance.

The Marquis de la Fayette (1757–1834) in his army uniform.

The Abbé Sieyès (1748–1836). He was elected to the Estates General in 1789 and remained active in politics throughout the revolution. However, he had a habit of keeping quiet when serious problems arose and he was called 'the mole of the revolution' because he vanished out of sight whenever there was trouble. In 1799 he helped to bring Napoleon Bonaparte to power.

Ma foimte, il étoit tems que je me réveillisse, car l'opréssion de mes fers me donnigns le cochemaq un peu trop fort.

A cartoon showing the nobility and clergy horrified at the awakening of the 'third estate' in 1789. The caption underneath read: 'My goodness, it is time I woke up, for my chains were giving me nightmares in my sleep'.

2   The Events of 1789

We saw in the previous section that 1789 was the year of hope for the people of France. They hoped that the Estates General would bring about great changes in the country that would give them a chance of a better life. They were not to be disappointed. The year 1789 was indeed one of great and revolutionary changes in France.

The Opening of the Estates General

During the early days of May, the deputies of the clergy, the nobility and the third estate, gathered in Versailles for the opening of the Estates General. On 4 May in wet and windy weather, the official opening ceremony took place with the celebration of High Mass in the Church of Saint-Louis. All the deputies had to walk in procession to the church, according to rules laid down by the king. The clergy were allowed to dress in their ordinary dress, with the bishops in their splendid robes. The nobility were allowed to dress in fine silk costumes, with feathered hats, and swords dangling at their sides. But the poor third estate had to march right at the front of the procession, separated from everybody else, and dressed in simple black clothes. This annoyed them, for it showed that the king thought them inferior to the nobility and the clergy.

The Third Estate stand firm

When the meetings of the Estates General began on the next day, the deputies of the third estate acted quickly. They refused to discuss anything until the nobility and clergy agreed to join with them in a single assembly. The nobility and clergy refused, because they knew that this would involve them in recognising the third estate as their equal. As a result of this refusal, no business was done during the whole month of May.

   In June, after more than a month of waiting, the third estate decided to take matters into their own hands. On 17 June they called themselves the

The first session of the Estates General in May 1789.

'National Assembly', and claimed that they spoke for the whole French nation. They then started to discuss plans for the reform of France. The man who suggested the name 'National Assembly', was the Abbé Sieyès, author of the pamphlet *What is the Third Estate?*

The Tennis Court Oath

The king was annoyed by all this. On 20 June, when the members of the National Assembly arrived at their meeting hall, they found the doors locked and barred. This had been done on the orders of the king. He wanted to stop the National Assembly from holding its meetings. As it was a rainy day, the members all took refuge in an indoor tennis court that stood nearby. There they took an oath that they would never stop meeting until they had completely reformed the government of France. This oath was called the Tennis Court Oath. It showed the king that the National Assembly was determined to continue its work. A week later the king realised this. He ordered the nobility and clergy to join the National Assembly.

The King takes action

To many people it seemed that the third estate had won all they wanted. Everyone now sat in one assembly and discussed reform together. But while

The Tennis Court Oath (20 June 1789).

this was going on, the king was secretly planning to get rid of the National Assembly. In early July he gave orders for troops to be sent to Paris and Versailles. He planned to use these to surround the hall where the assembly met, and force all the deputies to go home.

News of this plan reached the people of Paris on 12 July. It was a sunny Sunday afternoon. People were out in the streets and parks, enjoying the sun and the fresh air. When they heard the news they began to search frantically for arms so that they could defend Paris from attack. Crowds of people looted gun shops and raided arms stores, carrying off muskets, pistols and powder.

The Fall of the Bastille

The search for arms lasted several days, and on 14 July, crowds gathered around the Bastille, a fortress in the east of Paris. The Bastille had walls a hundred feet high and was surrounded by a deep and dangerous moat. In the

A picture of the attack on the Bastille. Note the white flag of surrender on the battlements at the top of the picture. On the left is the governor, de Launay, being taken away under arrest; he was later attacked and beheaded by the angry crowd.

31

old days it had been used as a special prison, but now there were only a few prisoners left there. (One of them was a Dublin man, John Whyte, who turned out to be completely mad.) However, although it held few prisoners, the Bastille did contain hundreds of guns and tons of gunpowder. The crowd knew this and so called on the governor to surrender.

At first the governor, de Launay, refused. He was confident that his men could defend the Bastille against any attack. However, while he was talking to the crowds from the top of the fortress walls, two people from the crowd slipped across the moat and let down the drawbridge. Immediately the crowd surged across the bridge and into the outer courtyard. Many of them were shot dead as the troops opened fire from the fortress walls. Once they had reached the courtyard, the crowd brought up cannon and aimed them at the doors of the fortress. The governor then agreed to surrender, and the Bastille was captured.

The fall of the Bastille was a great event. It was celebrated all over Europe, and 14 July is still a national holiday in France today. It meant that the king had no hope of silencing the French people, or of getting rid of the National Assembly. He therefore ordered all his troops to return to their barracks, and allowed the people of Paris to set up their own police force—the National Guard. La Fayette, the hero of the American War of Independence, was made the first commander of the National Guard. The king also agreed that the country should have a new flag, made up of white (the royal colour) and red and blue (the colours of Paris). This was the tricolour—the national flag of France today.

The Great Fear

The revolt in Paris was followed by revolts in other towns in France. Everywhere the royal officials were forced to give up their powers. They were replaced by new officials who had the confidence of the people. National Guards were also set up, as in Paris, to keep the peace.

In the countryside too the peasants rose up in revolt. We saw earlier that they lived in terrible poverty, and hoped that the third estate would solve their problems. Now, in July and August, they had a 'great fear' that the nobility would try to prevent the National Assembly in Paris from carrying out reforms. They also feared that the nobility would refuse to give up their feudal dues. So they took the law into their own hands, and invaded the homes of the nobility to destroy the manorial roles which contained the details of their feudal dues. Fires raged in many parts of France as the peasants burnt many noble houses to the ground. They won their case. On 4 August 1789 the National Assembly declared that feudalism would be abolished. The peasants had won a great victory.

The King comes to Paris

One final thing remained to be done, in order to make the revolution a complete success. The king and the National Assembly were still in Versailles, twelve miles outside Paris. The people of Paris were worried by this. They feared that the king might try to get rid of the National Assembly again. Therefore they wanted to have both the king and the National Assembly moved to Paris. That way the people of Paris could keep watch on the king and protect the National Assembly from harm.

In early October they saw their chance to do this. There was a shortage of bread in Paris. So, on 5 October, seven thousand women marched from Paris to Versailles. Once there, they decided to ask the king to return with them to Paris and take up residence there. Seven thousand women make a terrifying sight—even to a king! So Louis readily agreed to their request.

Next day a long procession slowly made its way to Paris. The procession

Another view of the fall of the Bastille.

Women on the way from Paris to Versailles on 5 October 1789.

was made up of thousands of women and some troops. In the middle of it was the royal coach carrying the king, the queen and their son. The women surrounded the coach, and shouted that they had 'the baker, the baker's wife and the baker's boy'. They knew that as long as the king was in Paris, they would never go short of food.

3 The Execution of the King

The exciting events of 1789 put an end to the old style of government in France. Everyone now wanted changes to be made that would give more power and freedom to ordinary people. It was up to the National Assembly to make these changes.

Who were the leading personalities in the National Assembly? Some of them we have already seen, such as the Abbé Sieyès and General La Fayette. Yet there were two others who soon made a name for themselves: Count Mirabeau and Maximilien Robespierre.

Count Mirabeau

Count Mirabeau was a huge, ugly man from the south of France. He had broad shoulders, a badly scarred face, and big, staring eyes. Strange stories were told about him. It was said that when he was born he already had two front teeth. His father thought he was extremely ugly as a young child, and once wrote to a friend: 'He is as ugly as Satan'. Certainly he was always in trouble, and often ended up in prison. Despite these troubles, he still managed to become famous as a writer of books and pamphlets. Because of this fame, he was elected as a member of the third estate in 1789, and his voice soon boomed out in the National Assembly. People did not always trust him, but they always listened to what he had to say.

Honoré Gabriel de Riquetti, Count Mirabeau (1749–91). Although he was a supporter of the Third Estate in 1789, Mirabeau soon accepted bribes from the king and began to work for him. Because of this he soon became unpopular and when he died in 1791 few people mourned him.

Maximilien Robespierre

Maximilien Robespierre was a very different sort of a person. Robespierre was a lawyer from the town of Arras in northern France. He was a small, thin person, who ate very little and drank even less. He dressed neatly, wore well-cut clothes, and always wore a small powdered wig. His voice was quiet, and he often had difficulty in making himself heard. Nevertheless, he always spoke up on behalf of the poor against the rich, for he had seen the problems of poverty in his home town of Arras. People did not always agree with what Robespierre said, but they had to admit that he was fearless and honest. Because of this they called him The Incorruptible. We shall see more of Robespierre later.

Maximilien Robespierre (1758–94), future leader of the Committee of Public Safety.

The National Assembly reforms France

Between 1789 and 1791 the National Assembly carried out many reforms. In August 1789 it drew up the Declaration of the Rights of Man. In this the Assembly made it clear that all men would be treated as equals, and that they would be allowed to have as much liberty as possible. The declaration started with the famous words: 'Men are born and remain free and equal in rights'. No government in Europe had ever said that before.

How was the country to be governed? The power to make laws and vote taxes was given to the Assembly elected by the people. The king was allowed to continue as the head of government, but he had to carry out the decisions of the Assembly. As for local government, that too was reformed. The old royal officers lost their powers and were replaced by specially elected councils. In this way the people of France were given complete control of their own affairs.

Other reforms were also carried out. Reforms were made in the law courts, and the Assembly began to draw up a more fair code of laws. All taxes on food were done away with, and the old medieval guilds were abolished. Most important of all, people were allowed to talk politics and discuss new ideas more freely then they had ever done before. Hundreds of newspapers were published, giving news and views on the work of the National Assembly. They were read in cafés, stuck up on the walls, or read

In the session of 4–5 August the National Assembly abolished feudalism and all other privileges. This made all men equal before the law and made life easier for the peasants.

aloud at street corners. People also joined clubs, so that they could discuss the new reforms. The most famous of these clubs was the Jacobin Club in Paris. This was just around the corner from where the National Assembly met, so that deputies could go there to listen to people's views, before going on to the Assembly to vote. Most other towns in France also had a Jacobin Club, where political affairs were discussed.

People hoped that all these reforms would bring peace and prosperity to France. However, they were wrong. Two problems soon arose which quickly brought war and destruction to the country.

The Reform of the Church

One problem arose over the question of reforming the Catholic Church in France. Most members of the National Assembly believed, like the thinkers of the Enlightenment, that the power of the Church should be reduced. So, in July 1790, they passed a law called the Civil Constitution of the Clergy. This stated that all bishops and priests would have to be elected by the people, just as all other state officials were. It also reduced the powers of the pope over the Church in France, and said that all clergy would have to take an oath of loyalty to the state.

Some of the clergy thought that this law interfered too much with the

Varennes.

affairs of the Church. The pope agreed. In March 1791 he told the French clergy not to co-operate with the reforms. As a result, Catholics in France were divided into two groups. Those who co-operated with the reforms tended to support the revolution. Those who obeyed the pope tended to oppose the revolution. So, for the first time, many ordinary people in France disapproved of the work of the National Assembly.

The royal family being stopped and arrested in Varennes. In the carriage are the king and queen and their son and daughter, looking out to see what has happened.

The King tries to escape

Another problem which worried the National Assembly was the attitude of the king towards the Revolution. Louis XVI disapproved of all the reforms that the National Assembly had carried out. He wanted to abolish them and to regain his former powers. In order to do this he decided to escape from France and to seek help from his brother-in-law, the Emperor of Austria, Leopold II. He hoped that the emperor would lend him his armies so that he

37

The return of the royal family to Paris. Note how the coach is surrounded by guards.

could invade France and get rid of the National Assembly. Then he would be able to abolish all the reforms and rule as he had done before the Revolution.

On the night of 21 June 1791 the king and queen tip-toed out of the royal palace and climbed into a waiting coach. The coach then left Paris and sped towards the frontier. All went well until the coach came to the small village of Varennes, a few miles away from the frontier with Belgium. The local postmaster recognised the king's face and raised the alarm. The local National Guard then stopped the coach and sent the king and queen back to Paris. When the coach arrived back in Paris, crowds of people lined the streets staring, angry and silent at the royal couple. Apparently the queen's hair turned grey from fright.

France goes to War
When he realised that Louis XVI had failed to escape from France, Emperor

Leopold II called a special meeting with King Frederick William II of Prussia. The two monarchs then made the Declaration of Pillnitz. In this they promised to help Louis XVI to regain his former powers. Most people in France were indignant at this promise. They accused Leopold of interfering in the internal affairs of France. Therefore, they demanded that France should go to war with Austria and force the emperor to withdraw his declaration. Louis XVI was quite happy to agree to this demand. He was confident that the Austrian armies would easily defeat the French, and restore him to his rightful authority.

On 20 April 1792 France declared war on Austria. Prussia joined sides with Austria and the French armies were soon forced to retreat. Defeat followed upon defeat until, in early August, Paris itself was in danger of falling to the enemy. Louis XVI was delighted by these defeats and refused to take any measures to strengthen the defences of Paris.

The Fall of the King

However, the people of Paris became annoyed at the king's attitude. So, on 10 August 1792, they rose up in revolt and attacked the royal palace. Louis XVI and Marie-Antoinette were forced to escape by a back door and were promptly put under arrest.

The executioner holds up the head of Louis XVI after his execution, to prove to the crowds that he is dead. Queen Marie-Antoinette was executed some months later.

In September 1792 a new assembly was elected, called the Convention. On 21 September the Convention abolished the monarchy and declared France a republic. Four months later they declared Louis XVI guilty of high treason and condemned him to death. On the cold and frosty morning of 21 January 1793 Louis XVI was taken to the Place de la Révolution in the middle of Paris. There he was beheaded by the guillotine.

4 The Reign of Terror

The execution of the king did not put an end to the troubles of France. On the contrary, there were worse troubles yet to come. Soon the guillotine that cut off the king's head would be used on many other people. The reign of Louis XVI was followed by the Reign of Terror.

Why did the troubles of France continue after the death of the king? To understand this we have to go back a little in time.

The Committee of Public Safety

Louis de Saint-Just (1767–94), close friend of Robespierre and member of the Committee of Public Safety.

You will remember that in September of 1792 a new assembly, called the Convention, was elected. This Convention had ordered the execution of the king. However, it also had the task of drawing up a new constitution for France, now that it had been declared a republic. This was a difficult task. It was made worse by the fact that France was still at war. In the early months of 1793 after the execution of the king, more and more countries joined Austria and Prussia in the war against France. Soon it became obvious that France would be defeated unless strong action was taken. So the Convention set up a special Committee of Public Safety to take emergency measures to save the country.

Saint-Just

The Committee of Public Safety had twelve members. The most famous of them was Maximilien Robespierre, whom we met earlier at the Estates General. Another member who worked closely with Robespierre was Saint-Just. Saint-Just was twenty-six years old and the son of a cavalry officer from north-eastern France. Women found him very handsome, but behind that good-looking face there was a ruthless streak. He hated all those who disagreed with him. Everyone who opposed the Revolution, he said, should be 'utterly destroyed'. He spent most of his time with the armies, encouraging soldiers to fight and planning attacks against the enemy.

Couthon

Georges-Auguste Couthon was also an important member of the Committee. Couthon came from the south of France and was crippled in both legs. Because of this he could not walk, and so moved himself around in a wooden wheelchair. (The wheelchair can still be seen today, in a museum in Paris). Couthon was a lawyer by trade, and before the revolution he defended many poor people in the law courts. When he was elected to the Committee of Public Safety he co-operated closely with Robespierre.

The 'Sans-Culottes' of Paris

All the members of the Committee of Public Safety were determined to make sure that France was not defeated in war. They were strongly supported by many of the poor people in the cities and towns of France. These people called themselves the *sans-culottes* (which meant 'without breeches'). This was because they wore baggy trousers rather than the fashionable knee-breeches that were worn by rich people. They were poor and proud of it. Some of them had fought to capture the Bastille in 1789. Others had helped to attack the Tuileries in August 1792. Now they supported Robespierre and his colleagues on the Committee of Public Safety.

What did the *sans-culottes* want the Committee to do? Well, firstly they wanted it to make sure that France did not lose the war. Secondly, they wanted it to improve food supplies and bring down prices, so that the poor could lead a more comfortable life. In short, they wanted a better deal for the poor.

The Committee of Public Safety saves France

The Committee took swift measures to improve the war situation. On 23 August 1793 it brought in a special law called the 'mass levy' which ordered everybody to work for the war effort. Young men were sent out to fight in the armies, and married men were told to work in arms factories. Old men were even told to walk about the streets, encouraging others to fight! At the same time, the Committee also replaced many of the older army generals with younger men. These younger generals often had more skill and more enthusiasm in battle. As a result of all these measures, French armies were soon victorious in the field.

The Committee also took action to help the poor. It made sure that supplies of grain and other foodstuffs were plentiful. It also passed a law called the 'general maximum' on 29 September 1793. This law fixed the prices that could be charged for all goods, and so kept down the cost of living.

Georges-Auguste Couthon (1755–94), holding in his hand a letter to Robespierre.

A typical sans-culotte, wearing baggy trousers and, on his head, a 'bonnet of liberty'.

The wife of a sans-culotte, armed to defend France against the enemy. Some women did get involved in politics during the revolution, but they were not always approved of. Robespierre, for example, said that a woman's place was in the home and he made sure that women did not establish political clubs. Women did not get the vote in France until 1946.

The Terror

Another problem that the Committee of Public Safety had to face was the problem of civil war. Many people in France had disagreed with the execution of the king, and opposed the work of the Committee of Public Safety. Some of them rose up in rebellion, especially in the west and south of the country.

The Committee, therefore, sent out strong armies to defeat the rebels. All those who were captured were put to death. In the west of France over seven thousand rebels were executed. Many of them died by drowning. They were chained together and put onto barges. The barges were then pushed out into the middle of the river Loire and deliberately sunk. No one survived. In the city of Lyons in southern France, over sixteen hundred people were executed. Many of them were lined up in front of their own graves and mowed down by cannon fire, so that they fell into their graves.

Apart from those people who actually rebelled against the Committee of Public Safety, there were others who plotted for its overthrow. These were regarded as traitors, and were dealt with by a special revolutionary tribunal in Paris. This sent over sixteen thousand people to the guillotine, including Marie-Antoinette, and many leading politicians.

Action against the Church

The Committee of Public Safety also took strong action against the Catholic Church. As we saw earlier in this chapter, many priests did not approve the reform of the Civil Constitution of the Clergy. Many of them supported the rebellion against the government. Soon the Committee of Public Safety and the *sans-culottes* thought that all priests were opponents of the Revolution. So, in October and November 1793 the sans-culottes closed down churches all over France, and used them as meeting halls or grain stores. Many priests went into hiding, and many others gave up the priesthood and married.

A new calendar for France

Even the calendar was changed, so that all memories of Christianity would be forgotten. Sunday was abolished, and the week was made ten days long. The names of the months were abolished and replaced by new names which described the seasons. Even the years were changed, so that they counted from the year when the king was overthrown (1792). The year 1792–3 became year I, 1793–4 became year II, and so on. These changes confused many people, but they were meant to show that a completely new age had started in the history of man.

42

The Fall of the Committee

By the summer of 1794 the Committee of Public Safety had achieved a great deal. French Armies were victorious everywhere, the civil war had been ended, and the Terror had rid France of many enemies.

However, the Committee did not last much longer. All of its members had worked extremely hard, and were now tired and weary. As the hot summer wore on, they began to quarrel with one another. Robespierre became extremely irritable and complained in the Convention about the behaviour of his colleagues. Some people in the Convention saw this as their chance to get rid of the Committee. Many of them wanted an end to the Terror. Others feared that the Committee was becoming too powerful.

So, on 24 July 1794 Robespierre was arrested along with Saint-Just and Couthon. Robespierre then tried to shoot himself, but only managed to break his jaw. Couthon struggled from his wheelchair and threw himself through a window. Yet he only suffered from cuts and bruises. Saint-Just remained dignified to the end.

The end was not long in coming. Next day, 28 July 1794, all three were guillotined. Soon the Committee of Public Safety was abolished and the Terror came to an end. The most terrifying period in the history of the Revolution was over.

Georges Jacques Danton (1759–94). He was a lawyer who became a politician during the revolution and was extremely popular with the people of Paris. He was a member of the Jacobins and, for a while, friendly with Robespierre. However, in the winter of 1973–4 he began to complain that Robespierre's policies were too harsh and extreme; as a result he was arrested and guillotined in the spring of 1794.

TO DO

1 You are a visitor to the palace of Versailles. Write a letter to a friend telling him (or her) about the gardens, the palace, and the king and queen. Use the pictures at the beginning of this chapter to help you to do this.

2 Suggest some ways in which Louis XVI could have prevented the Revolution from happening.

3 You are a newspaper reporter sitting in a café near the Bastille on 14 July 1789. Write a report about the fall of the Bastille, and the behaviour of the crowd.

4 You are one of the members of the third estate of the Estates General. Write a diary about the events that you saw between May and October 1789.

5 Take another look at the reforms carried out in France between 1789 and 1791. Which of them do you consider to have been the most important?

6 You are one of the secretaries of the Committee of Public Safety. Write a diary about the events of the Terror. Put down in your diary what it was like to work with Robespierre and his colleagues.

7 Stage a debate between the ghost of Louis XVI and the ghost of Robespierre. Try to decide which of them was the better ruler of France.

Jean-Paul Marat (1743–93). He was a journalist who, in his paper *L'Ami du Peuple* (the Friend of the People), called for the death of all those who opposed the revolution. Many people disliked him for this and on 13 July 1793 a young girl, Charlotte Corday, stabbed him to death while he was taking a bath.

TO READ
The French Revolution, Then and There Series, M. Rosenthal, Longman Group.
The Tale of Two Cities, C. Dickens.
The French Revolution (i) The Fall of the Bastille, Jackdaw Series no. 57, Jackdaw Publications.
The French Revolution (ii) The Terror, Jackdaw Series no. 58, Jackdaw Publications.

DATELINE
1789   May: meeting of the Estates General.
         June: the Tennis Court Oath.
         July: the fall of the Bastille.
         October: Louis XVI is taken to Paris.
1790   The Civil Constitution of the Clergy.
1792   France declares war.
1793   Execution of Louis XVI.
1793–4 The Committee of Public Safety rules France.

The arrest of Robespierre.

3   The Age of Napoleon, 1799–1815

After the French Revolution was over, France was ruled by Napoleon Bonaparte.
You have probably heard of Napoleon. He was a clever and ambitious man. He was
also one of the most powerful rulers that the world has ever seen.

In this chapter you will find out how Napoleon came to power. You will also
discover how he ruled France and conquered most of the countries of Europe.

Napoleon Bonaparte (1769–1821).

Napoleon as a soldier during the revolution.

1 Napoleon comes to power

After the Committee of Public Safety had been abolished, no government was strong enough to rule France properly. In 1795 a new constitution was voted which gave power to five men, called the Directors. This period of rule was known as the Directory, and lasted from 1795–99.

The Directory fails to govern France

It was hoped that the Directory would bring peace and prosperity to France. However, it failed to do this because it was not strong enough to keep law and order. Many people disobeyed the laws, and some plotted to overthrow the Directory by force. All the time prices continued to rise, and the poor people had to struggle to keep alive. What France needed was strong government. But where would such government come from?

The Victories of the French Armies

The answer was—the army. During the period of the Directory, the French armies won many victories abroad. They conquered Holland, Belgium, Switzerland, Italy, and parts of Germany. These conquests made France into the most powerful country in Europe. They also made the army commanders into extremely important people. One such commander was Napoleon Bonaparte. He was the person who brought the Directory to an end, and provided France with strong government.

The Early Years of Napoleon

Who was Napoleon Bonaparte? He was born on the island of Corsica on 15 August 1769, the son of a poor nobleman. Corsica had just come under French rule, so that at the age of ten, Napoleon went to France for his education. He went to military colleges where he worked hard and did extremely well. His teachers remarked that he was very intelligent and quick to learn. He soon proved how right they were.

At the age of sixteen he went into the French army as a lieutenant of artillery. At first he was not happy. His fellow officers made fun of him because he was poor. They jeered at him because he was short. They burst out laughing whenever he spoke, because of his strong Corsican accent. Soon Napoleon came to hate the French. He longed for the day that he could return to Corsica and free it from French rule.

Napoleon and the Revolution

However, when the Revolution broke out he changed many of his ideas. He quickly became a supporter of the Committee of Public Safety and was

Napoleon as commander of the French armies in Italy.

a close friend of Robespierre's brother. This friendship nearly cost him his life, for after Robespierre was executed in 1794, Napoleon was put in prison. Nevertheless, the government soon released him and allowed him to return to his post in the army.

Victory and Fame

In 1796 Napoleon gained promotion. He was made commander of the French armies in Italy. In 1796 and 1797 he led his army to brilliant victories

The Battle of the Pyramids (22 July 1798).

and brought the whole of Italy under the control of France. In 1798 he followed up these successes by sailing with his army to Egypt. There he defeated the Egyptian forces in the Battle of the Pyramids and entered Cairo in triumph. These successes made Napoleon famous throughout Europe. Everyone agreed that he must be quite an outstanding general and inspiring leader.

Napoleon takes command

Yet Napoleon had ambitions that went beyond mere victories in battle. In the summer of 1799, while still in Egypt, he heard that people in France were getting more and more dissatisfied with the Directory. So, Napoleon hurried back to Paris. There he had discussions with people who wanted to replace the Directory with a stronger government. One of these people was the Abbé Sieyès, who in 1789 had written the famous pamphlet *What is the Third Estate?* Sieyès persuaded Napoleon to co-operate with him. The two men then gained the co-operation of a third man, the politician Roger Ducos. Together they planned the downfall of the Directory.

On 9 November 1799 the three men persuaded the Directors to resign. Next day they had themselves appointed as Consuls, with the task of drawing up a new constitution for France. Few people dared to protest against this seizure of power, for Napoleon had the support of the army.

From Consul to Emperor

At this stage Napoleon shared power with the two other consuls, Sieyès and Ducos. However, he soon showed that he intended to rule France alone. In 1800 he held a referendum. He asked the people of France to vote him into office as First Consul for the next ten years. They did. Two years later he asked them to vote him into office as First Consul for the rest of his life. They did. Finally, in 1804, he asked them to vote him Emperor of France. They did so by a massive majority.

On 2 December 1804, in the Cathedral of Notre Dame, Napoleon was crowned Emperor of France. The pope came from Rome to perform the ceremony. However, when the time came for the pope to place the crown on Napoleon's head, Napoleon took it from him. Slowly but surely he placed

Napoleon as First Consul in 1800.

Napoleon's coronation as emperor.

the crown on his own head. In this way he showed the world that he owed his success to no-one. He was a self-made man.

2 Napoleon and France

What sort of a man was Napoleon Bonaparte, the new ruler of France? Remember that in 1799, when he came to power, he was still only thirty-one years old. Everyone knew that he was a brilliant general, but soon they saw that he was also a clever politician.

A Day in the Life of Napoleon

One of the secrets of his success was his hard work. He used to get up at seven in the morning and do two hours work before breakfast. After breakfast he returned to his desk, reading letters and dictating orders to his secretaries. During the fifteen years that he ruled France, he dictated more than eighty thousand letters and orders. After a light lunch, the afternoon was spent discussing affairs of state with his ministers. Often he spent this part of the day with his Council of State, as we shall see later.

In the evenings Napoleon ate a solid dinner; often it was a state banquet, or a reception for a foreign diplomat. After this he would either go to the theatre, or retire to his room and continue his work. He then went to bed quite early, usually at around ten o'clock. However, like many clever people, Napoleon was not a good sleeper. He often spent hours awake in bed. At other times he got up in the middle of the night and wandered around Paris, dressed in the clothes of a working man. He could then talk to ordinary people without them knowing who he was. In this way, he could find out what working people thought of himself and his government. He was not always pleased by what he heard.

Napoleon did not merely work hard; he was also very intelligent. He knew how to deal with people, in order to get what he wanted from them. The result was always the same: people did as he wished. His ability to persuade people in this way had made him into a good general. Now it made him a strong ruler.

The Empress Josephine (1763–1814). One of the prettiest women of her time she lost her first husband, an army general, when he was guillotined in 1794. In 1796 she married Napoleon, but it was never a happy marriage and they had no children. Partly because of this, Napoleon divorced her in 1810 and married an Austrian princess, Marie Louise, who bore him a son in 1811.

Charles Maurice de Talleyrand (1754–1838).

Reforms in Government

How did Napoleon govern France? He started by appointing about forty people to a Council of State. The Council of State had important duties to perform. It discussed Napoleon's decisions, drew up new laws, and looked after the running of the country. Next to Napoleon, it was the centre of government. Napoleon, therefore, chose some of the cleverest men in France as his councillors.

Talleyrand and Fouché

Two of these men were particularly important. One was Charles Maurice de Talleyrand. Talleyrand had been a bishop before the Revolution of 1789. However, when the Revolution broke out, he changed his mind and became a diplomat instead. During the Terror, Talleyrand was away from France on diplomatic business. However, he later returned, and helped Napoleon to take over power in 1799. Napoleon then made him Minister for Foreign Affairs. Talleyrand was ugly, but he was also clever and cunning. No one knew as much about foreign affairs as he did, and it was for this reason that Napoleon appointed him to the Council of State. However, Napoleon did not trust him, for Talleyrand was never loyal to anyone. In 1807 he resigned from the Council of State and helped to plot Napoleon's downfall.

Joseph Fouché was a schoolteacher from the prosperous town of Nantes in the west of France. He had been a strong supporter of the Revolution in 1789, and had worked closely with Robespierre during the Terror. Like Talleyrand, Fouché had helped Napoleon to take over power in 1799.

Joseph Fouché (1759–1820), Napoleon's Minister of Police.

Pius VII, pope from 1800–1823. He signed the Concordat with Napoleon and later attended his coronation as emperor in 1804.

Because of this Napoleon made him Minister of Police. Fouché quickly set up an efficient spy system, and his spies reported to him on everything that went on in the country. Thus Fouché was able to warn Napoleon when people were plotting against his government. However, Napoleon later came to distrust Fouché, and so dismissed him in 1810. Fouché then helped Talleyrand to plot Napoleon's downfall.

The Prefects

The Council of State helped Napoleon to make important decisions. However, these decisions had to be put into effect throughout France. So, in order to make sure that this was done, Napoleon appointed special government officials called Prefects. There was one prefect for every region of France. They made sure that the government's commands were obeyed, and they looked after the affairs in their own region. Every month they wrote a report on how things were going in their region, and they sent this report to Paris. In this way the Council of State could find out how people felt about its decisions.

Napoleon used the Council of State and the prefects to make many changes in France. He was determined to restore order in the country and to make his government strong.

The Concordat and the Catholic Church

One of his greatest successes was to solve the problem of religion. You will remember that during the Revolution many changes were made in the Catholic Church by the Civil Constitution of the Clergy. (Chapter 2, sections 3 and 4). Many Catholics had opposed these changes and had become opponents of the Revolution. They wanted to have their religion restored and they wanted to see the monarchy back in France. Napoleon was worried by this. He saw that he needed the support of French Catholics. Therefore, he decided to negotiate a settlement with the pope, which would restore the Catholic religion in France, and make all Catholics loyal to him.

Negotiations soon started and in July 1801 Pope Pius VII and Napoleon signed an agreement called the Concordat. In this the pope allowed Napoleon to appoint all the bishops in France. He also agreed that the clergy should take an oath of loyalty to Napoleon. In return Napoleon agreed that his government would pay the clergy's wages. He also agreed to make sure that Catholics could practise their religion freely throughout France.

The Concordat was a great triumph for Napoleon. It gave him the support of the pope, and so meant that most of the Catholics in France would support him. This success encouraged him to make similar Concordats

The Civil Code of 1804. This still forms the basis of many of the laws of France today, and of those of many other countries.

CODE CIVIL

DES

FRANÇAIS.

ÉDITION ORIGINALE ET SEULE OFFICIELLE.

GRAND JUGE ET MINISTRE DE LA JUSTICE.

À PARIS,

DE L'IMPRIMERIE DE LA RÉPUBLIQUE.

AN XII. 1804.

with other Churches, especially with the Lutherans, Calvinists, and Jews. He promised them that they could practise their religion freely. In return they promised to encourage their members to be obedient to Napoleon.

Napoleon and Schools

By solving the religious problem Napoleon became very popular. However, he also carried out other reforms which made him well liked by the people. For example he issued a code of laws in 1804, called the Civil Code. This clearly stated what the law was, and what people were allowed to do. He also improved the system of education. He encouraged the religious orders to set up schools for very young children. He established state schools (called *lycées*) for older children. Finally, he also established a special government ministry, called the Imperial University. This looked after the appointment of teachers. It also controlled what was taught in the schools. In this way even schoolboys came to hear of Napoleon, and they learnt that it was their duty to obey him.

By these reforms, and by many others, Napoleon provided strong government for France. Soon the country prospered and the troubles of the Revolution were forgotten.

Usage des Nouvelles Mesures.

France first began to use metric measurements during the revolution. This poster, printed in 1800, explains the use of measures such as the litre (instead of the pint), the gramme (instead of the pound) and the metre (instead of the yard).

One of Napoleon's most famous army commanders, Marshall Ney, (1769–1815).

3 Napoleon and Europe

Most historians now agree that Napoleon was not just interested in ruling France. He also wanted to become the most powerful ruler in Europe. For a short while he succeeded in doing this. His victories in battle brought him power that was beyond his wildest dreams. What was the secret of his success?

The French Armies

Part of Napoleon's success was due to the quality of the French armies. They were the best in Europe. The infantry soldiers were equipped with modern muskets that could fire accurately for long distances. The artillery had light field guns that could be moved about quickly on the field of battle. In addition to this French armies were huge, with over a million soldiers on active service. Most of them were experienced in battle, for France had been at war since 1792. Finally, Napoleon had very able generals in command of his troops. Most of them had risen from the ranks like himself. They were young, and all of them were loyal to France and her emperor.

Napoleon as Commander

However, although Napoleon had good armies, much of his success was due to his own skill as a commander. He trained his armies to march quickly, and to move into battle formation at a moment's notice. In this way he often surprised enemy armies by his speed and attacked them before they were ready. He also kept his cavalry units well trained. Many a battle was won when Napoleon sent his cavalry round the side of the enemy armies to attack them from the rear. In addition, Napoleon also had a special unit of his best troops, called the Imperial Guard. They were trained for emergencies, and Napoleon often used them to make the decisive breakthrough in a battle.

Another of Napoleon's commanders, Jean-Baptiste Bernadotte, (1763 –1844). He was elected King of Sweden in 1810 and his descendants are the royal family of Sweden still today.

Joachim Murat (1767–1815), a friend of Napoleon from his early days. A brilliant cavalry commander, he married Napoleon's sister in 1800, and in 1808 was made King of Naples. He was executed after Napoleon's fall from power in 1815.

The Battle of Austerlitz (2 December 1805).

Opposite (top)
The Battle of Jena (14 October 1806).

Opposite (bottom)
The Battle of Eylau against the Russians in 1807 was one of the toughest that Napoleon ever had to face. It took place in late winter when the weather was still bitterly cold and snow was thick on the ground. Here, Napoleon urges his men on for the final attack.

Above all, Napoleon was successful because he worked out his battle tactics well in advance. Often he spent days before a battle planning every move in detail. For Napoleon, every battle was like a game of chess, and he rarely lost.

Victories in Europe

By his victories in battle, Napoleon made himself master of Europe. In 1805 he defeated the Austrian armies in the battles of Ulm and Austerlitz. In 1806 he defeated the Prussians at Jena and Auerstadt. In 1807 he gained victories over the Russians in the battles of Eylau and Friedland. Not content with this, he then sent his troops into Spain and Portugal, to establish his power there. It seemed that no one could stop him.

By 1810, when Napoleon was at the height of his power, he had made his brothers Kings of Spain, Holland and Westphalia. His brother-in-law was King of Italy. Austria and Prussia obeyed his will. The whole of Europe seemed to be at his command.

The Struggle against Britain

However, one country still held out against him. That country was Britain. Ever since Napoleon had come to power, Britain had been one of his major enemies. The British government had constantly opposed his plans, and had often encouraged others to go to war against him. This made him determined to conquer Britain.

But how could Britain be conquered? At first Napoleon hoped that it could be done by sailing his army across the Channel and invading the south of England. However, by 1805 he realised that the British navy was strong

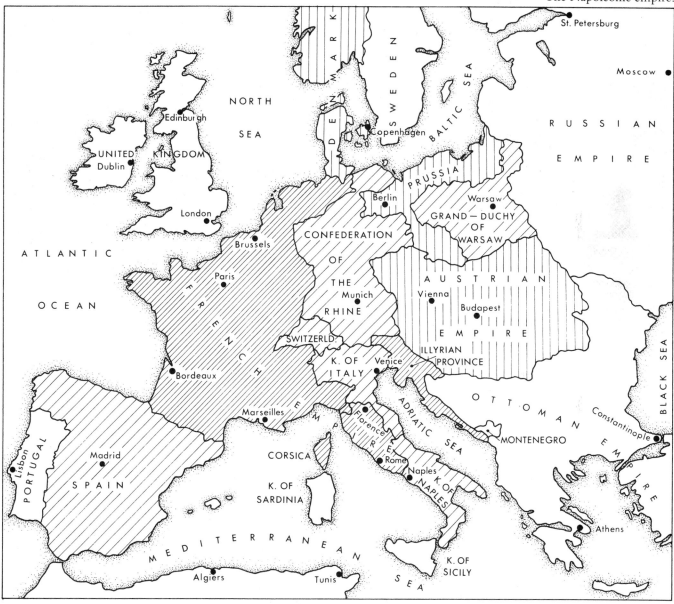

Opposite

Napoleon's invasion of Spain was not popular with the Spanish people. Many of them formed 'guerilla' bands and attacked the French armies; they were helped by a small force of English troops led by the Duke of Wellington. The French armies retaliated by executing many guerillas and also anyone who was suspected of co-operating with them. In these pictures a famous Spanish painter of the time, Goya, shows just how brutal some of these executions were.

States under direct French rule.

States under indirect French rule.

Allies of France.

The battle of Trafalgar, fought off the coast of Spain between the British and French fleets in October 1805. The British victory here was decisive. The French lost twenty of their best ships and all hopes of an invasion of England had to be shelved.

enough to prevent him doing this. He was proven right for on 21 October 1805 the British fleet, led by Admiral Nelson, defeated the French fleet at the Battle of Trafalgar. This ended all hopes of an invasion of Britain.

Napoleon then tried a different tactic. He decided to force Britain to surrender to him by ruining their trade. 'The British', he said, 'are a nation of shopkeepers'. These shopkeepers would soon give in to him if they could no longer buy and sell their goods. So in 1806 he started what was called the Continental System. He banned all trade between Britain and the other countries of Europe. Because he ruled most of Europe he was able to make sure that this ban was obeyed.

Despite the Continental System many British products were smuggled into Europe. Whenever they were discovered they were publicly burnt.

60

Napoleon defeating the Russian armies at the Battle of Borodino, just before his entry into Moscow (September 1812).

The Invasion of Russia

By 1810, when Napoleon was in command of most of Europe, the Continental System was beginning to work. The British found that they could no longer sell goods to Europe, and so their trade began to fall. However, there was one problem for Napoleon. The Tsar of Russia, Alexander I, refused to co-operate in the Continental System. This allowed Russian merchants to carry on their normal trade with Britain. Napoleon therefore decided that he would have to invade Russia, defeat the Russian armies, and then force the Tsar to co-operate. The invasion of Russia was the greatest gamble of his whole career. It was also the cause of his downfall.

To Moscow and back

In the summer of 1812 Napoleon crossed the border into Russia. He took with him an army of almost half a million men. The Russian armies slowly retreated in front of him. Occasionally they stopped to give battle for a short

The retreat from Russia. Two of the thousands of soldiers who died from Russian attacks or from cold or starvation, on the way back from Moscow.

while, and then they retreated again. In this way the Russian commander, Kutusov, hoped to keep his army intact. He knew that if he took on Napoleon in a full battle, he would lose. If he managed to keep his army together, he could live to fight another day. On 14 September 1812, Napoleon finally entered Moscow. It should have been a day of triumph, but it was not. The city was deserted. The Tsar and his government had left to join their army beyond Moscow. They refused to surrender and they refused even to negotiate. To make things worse for Napoleon, on the very day that he entered Moscow, the Tsar's agents set it on fire. For five days the flames raged, and the city was soon a smouldering ruin.

What could Napoleon do? He could not go on beyond Moscow in search of the Tsar. Winter was fast approaching and he knew that his army was not equipped for frost and heavy snow. So instead he decided to retreat back the way he had come. The retreat was a disaster. The snow and frost came earlier

than expected so that many thousands of troops died of cold and starvation. Thousands more were killed by Russian Cossack troops who harried the French all the way to the border. By the time that Napoleon finally struggled out of Russia with his army, he had only fifty thousand troops left.

The Battle of Waterloo (18 June 1815), Napoleon's last defeat.

The Fall of Napoleon

Tsar Alexander I was determined not to let the affair end there. He called on other European countries to join with him so that they could defeat Napoleon once and for all. Austria, Prussia and Britain quickly agreed, and became the allies of the Tsar. Napoleon decided not to surrender without a fight. He raised new armies and fought a brilliant defensive campaign against the allies. However, he was gradually forced to retreat back into France and finally surrendered in April 1814. For the first time in his life Napoleon had to admit defeat.

The allies were now faced with a difficult problem. What could they do with Napoleon? They were determined that he should not be allowed to rule France, as he was too dangerous. So instead, they sent him into exile, to the small island of Elba in the Mediterranean. There, in the middle of no-where, he was to spend the rest of his days. He was forbidden ever to leave Elba, but was allowed to live there in perfect freedom.

An officer of the Imperial Guard. You will see him in full colour on the front of this book.

The Return from Elba

That should have been the end of the story of Napoleon. However, it was not.

63

A portion of Napoleon's will.

Opposite (bottom)
Arthur Wellesley, Duke of Wellington (1769–1852). He fought against Napoleon in Spain and Portugal from 1808 onwards and in 1815 commanded the British forces at the Battle of Waterloo. He was also a politician and from 1828–30 was Prime Minister of Britain. He was a conservative who disliked change; in 1828 he accepted Catholic Emancipation in Britain and Ireland only under strong pressure, and he always opposed demands for the reform of Parliament.

Napoleon on the way to exile in St Helena. Compare this picture of him with those of him in his younger days; he looks much older and much fatter.

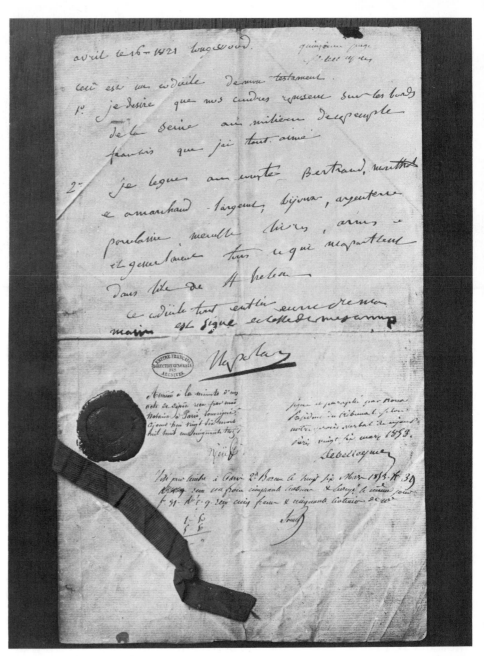

Napoleon quickly became bored with life on Elba, and decided to escape. In February 1815 he sailed to France and returned to Paris in triumph. The crowds cheered and Napoleon once more became Emperor of France.

Waterloo and Exile

However, his triumph was not to last long. On 18 June 1815, the allied armies led by the Duke of Wellington, defeated him at the Battle of Waterloo. This time Napoleon was sent into exile to the rocky island of St. Helena. There he spent the rest of his days in captivity. He died in 1821.

People have never forgotten Napoleon Bonaparte. Even after his death songs were written about him and people told stories about his most famous battles. For fifteen years he had been master of France and Europe. No one could forget that.

TO DO

1 Pretend that you are the wife of Napoleon Bonaparte. Write a short account of what it was like to live with him.
2 You are one of the soldiers in Napoleon's army. Write a diary of your life from the campaign in Italy (in 1796) until the Battle of Waterloo.
3 Take a map of Napoleon's Europe in 1810 and compare it with the map of Europe in 1760. What are the main differences? Now compare the same map with a map of modern Europe. What modern countries were within Napoleon's Empire?
4 Ask your teacher if you may hear a recording of Tchaikovsky's *1812 Overture*. Listen for the *Marseillaise* and for the sound of cannon fire.
5 The Duke of Wellington was born in Dublin. Find out more about him, and how he won the Battle of Waterloo.

After Napoleon's defeat in 1815 politicians from the countries that had defeated him met at Vienna to redraw the map of Europe. This meeting was called the Congress of Vienna, and it was decided to re-establish most of the states and countries that Napoleon had swept away.

Europe after the Congress of Vienna.

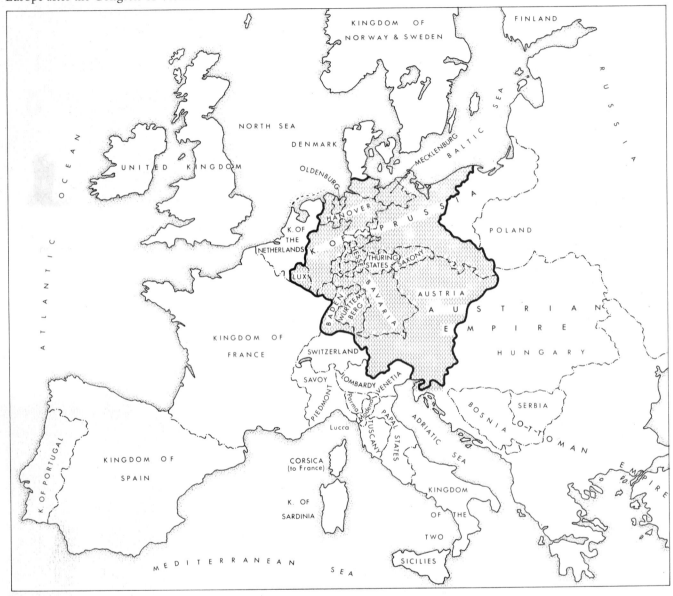

— Boundary of the German Confederation

TO READ
Napoleon, Richard Musman, Hutchinson.
Wellington's Army, Then and There Series, P. F. Speed, Longman Group.
The Gun, C. S. Forester.

The Battle of Trafalgar, Jackdaw Series no. 1, Jackdaw Publications.
The Battle of Waterloo, Jackdaw Series no. 18, Jackdaw Publications.
The Rise of Napoleon, Jackdaw Series no. 71, Jackdaw Publications.

DATELINE

1769	Napoleon born in Corsica.
1795–9	The Directory rules France.
1799	Napoleon seizes power.
1800	Napoleon becomes First Council.
1801	Napoleon negotiates the Concordat with the pope.
1804	Napoleon crowns himself Emperor of France.
1805	Battles of Ulm and Austerlitz.
1806	Battles of Jena and Auerstadt.
1807	Battles of Eylau and Friedland.
1812	Napoleon invades Russia.
1814	Napoleon banished to Elba.
1815	Battle of Waterloo: Napoleon banished to the island of St. Helena.
1821	Napoleon dies.

Field-marshal Prince von Blücher (1742–1819), commander of the Prussian forces at Waterloo.

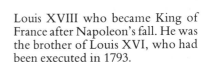

Joseph Bonaparte (1768–1844). Napoleon made him King of Spain in 1808, but he was never happy there, and after Napoleon's defeat in 1815 Joseph lost his throne and went to the United States where he stayed until his death.

Louis XVIII who became King of France after Napoleon's fall. He was the brother of Louis XVI, who had been executed in 1793.

One of Napoleon's brothers, Jerome Bonaparte, with his wife. Jerome was King of Westphalia.

4 The Unification of Italy and Germany, 1815–70

Between 1815 and 1870 two new countries arose in Europe. Those two countries were Italy and Germany. Of course, Italy and Germany had always existed. But they had previously been divided up into many small states which were independent of each other. By 1870 these small states, in both Italy and Germany, had been united into single countries.

In this chapter you will discover how this happened. You will read about the work of great men, such as Cavour, Garibaldi and Bismarck. These men unified Italy and Germany.

1 The Unification of Italy

If you look at a map of modern Europe, you will see that Italy is a united country. It is ruled from Rome by a single government. This was not always so. For many hundreds of years Italy was divided up into many small states. Each state was independent, with its own ruler and its own laws. People certainly thought of themselves as being Italians, but they were loyal to the ruler of their own particular state. They saw no reason for any change.

However, during the nineteenth century Italy became united. All the small states were united into the large country that we know today. How did this happen?

Napoleon and Italy

It all began with Napoleon. You will remember that Napoleon conquered Italy. After he did so, he abolished all the small states and then divided Italy into three parts. One part was ruled by France. Another part was called the Kingdom of Naples. The third part was called the Kingdom of Italy. Many Italians were grateful to Napoleon for getting rid of their old rulers. They hoped that he would follow this up by uniting the whole of Italy into one kingdom. However, he did not do this. He preferred to keep Italy divided so that he could rule it more easily.

Austria opposes Unity

In 1815, after Napoleon was defeated, all the old states of Italy were set up again. The old princes returned to their thrones. None of them were interested in uniting Italy. To make things worse, two of the Italian states—

Klemens von Metternich (1773–1859). Born in western Germany, Metternich became Foreign Minister of Austria in 1809 and Chancellor in 1821. He was one of Napoleon's most important opponents and, after Napoleon's fall in 1815, was determined to prevent the growth of nationalism and of political reform. He organised an effective secret police and, when necessary, obtained support from other countries to suppress rebellions in Italy and Spain. In 1848, when revolution broke out in Austria, he fled the country and went to England; although he returned to Austria in 1849 he took no part in active politics.

Lombardy and Venetia—were part of the Austrian Empire. Austria was a large country which contained many different peoples and nationalities. The Chancellor of Austria, Prince von Metternich, was therefore against the idea of Italian unity. He knew that if Italy became united, all the other nationalities in the Austrian Empire would also want to become united and independent. If this happened Austria would be destroyed. So Metternich was determined to imprison anyone who even talked about unifying Italy. As a result, many Italian nationalists were put into prison.

Giuseppe Mazzini

Despite the opposition of Metternich there were still a few people who hoped that Italy could be united. One of these people was Giuseppe Mazzini who came from Genoa. Mazzini believed that the only way to unify Italy was to drive the Austrians out of Lombardy and Venetia. Therefore in 1831 he took part in a rebellion against Austrian rule. The rebellion failed, and Mazzini was ordered to leave Italy. He went to live in London where he wrote many books about Italy. He also founded a society called Young Italy, to interest people in Italian unity. He was a quiet man who always dressed in black clothes to show that he was mourning for Italy. He smoked hundreds of cigars, and was also fond of budgerigars. Many of them fluttered around his small dark room in London.

Giuseppe Garibaldi

Giuseppe Garibaldi was a very different sort of person. He was a fighter rather than a thinker. While he was still quite a young man he joined the

Camillo Benso, Count di Cavour (1810–61).

Young Italy society organised by Mazzini. In 1834 he was ordered to leave Italy because he had taken part in a rebellion against Austrian rule. He went to South America. There he fought in several armies and became a famous military commander. Yet, all the time he was waiting for a chance to return to his home country of Italy. He wanted to fight for Italian unity.

Revolts in 1848–49

In 1848 it seemed that Mazzini and Garibaldi would have the chance to unify their country. Riots broke out in Sicily and soon spread to the rest of Italy. People everywhere rose up against their rulers and against the Austrian armies. Soon the Austrians were driven completely out of Italy, and Mazzini and Garibaldi returned in triumph. They went to Rome and began to make plans to unite the whole country under one government.

However, they did not act quickly enough. In 1849 the rioting began to die down and the Austrian armies returned. Mazzini and Garibaldi had to escape from Rome and go into exile again. The old rulers returned to their thrones and many people who had taken part in the rebellion were executed.

Camillo Benso di Cavour

Most people now gave up all hope of uniting Italy. They saw that Austria wanted to keep Italy divided. They also saw that the Italians by themselves were not strong enough to defeat the Austrian armies. However, they need not have despaired. Soon a man would appear on the scene who would overcome these difficulties. That man was Count Camillo Benso di Cavour.

Cavour was the Prime Minister of Piedmont, a state in northern Italy. He was a stout person with a handsome face, thick black hair, and wore steel-rimmed glasses. He was also very rich. Not only was he a farmer, but he was also a banker and the director of a railway company. Cavour was not really interested in uniting Italy. His real ambition in life was to make the state of Piedmont more powerful. To do this he wanted to drive the Austrians out of north Italy. Then Piedmont could take over the small states of Parma, Modena, Tuscany, Lombardy and Venetia.

Plombières and Villafranca

However, Cavour knew that the Piedmont army was too weak to take on the Austrian armies alone. Therefore, he decided to get help from France. He met Napoleon III, Emperor of France, at the small town of Plombières in 1858. There, he persuaded Napoleon III to send the French armies to his aid in a war against Austria.

War broke out in April 1859. Piedmont attacked Austria and, with the

The Unification of Italy.

Napoleon III, Emperor of France 1852–70. Nephew of the famous Napoleon Bonaparte, Napoleon III had supported the cause of Italian unity during his youth. After coming to power he did nothing about it until, in January 1858, a young Italian called Felice Orsini tried to blow up his coach while he was on his way to a night out at the opera. The explosion missed Napoleon III and Orsini was executed for his attempt, but the incident made Napoleon take an interest in the Italian cause and led to his meeting at Plombières with Cavour in 1858.

help of the French armies, gained a resounding victory at the Battle of Villafranca. Austria quickly decided to surrender Lombardy to Piedmont. A year later, in 1860 Parma, Modena and Tuscany also decided to join up with Piedmont. Piedmont now ruled almost the whole of northern Italy.

This was as far as Cavour wanted to go. He did not want to take over the small states in the centre of Italy that belonged to the pope. He knew that this would annoy Catholics all over Europe. Neither did he wish to take over the southern states of Sicily and Naples. Both of them were poor and barren states that would be difficult to govern.

Garibaldi and the Redshirts

Garibaldi at the head of his redshirt troops.

Victor Emmanuel II (1820–78). King of Piedmont from 1849 and King of Italy from 1861. He had firm faith in Cavour and also knew Garibaldi well.

However, there was one man who disagreed with Cavour. This was the old warrior Garibaldi, whom we last saw in the revolt of 1848–49. Garibaldi was now living in Piedmont, and he thought that Cavour should have gone on to unite the whole of Italy. Therefore he decided to take the matter into his own hands. He raised his own army of a thousand men, which he called his redshirts. He then set sail for Sicily. In May 1860 Garibaldi and the redshirts landed in Sicily and quickly conquered the island. From Sicily they crossed to Naples and conquered that also. Garibaldi then offered both states to the King of Piedmont, Victor Emmanuel II. Although Cavour was annoyed at what Garibaldi had done, he advised the king to accept.

Venetia and Rome

Italy was now almost completely united, except for the states of Venetia and Rome. Venetia was still ruled by Austria, and Rome by the pope. In 1866 Italy joined Prussia in a war against Austria. The Prussian armies defeated Austria at the Battle of Sadowa, and Austria promptly surrendered Venetia to Italy. Next it was the turn of Rome. The pope did not wish to give up his rule of Rome and had a garrison of French troops to protect the city against possible invasion. However, in 1870, France went to war with Prussia. As a result the French troops were recalled to France and Rome was left undefended. The Italian armies promptly took their chance. They captured Rome and made it the capital of Italy. The unification of Italy was now complete. A new nation was born.

The unity of Italy was made possible by the work of three great men. Mazzini wrote about it, Garibaldi fought for it and Cavour made it possible. However, even when Italy had been unified much work remained to be done. The north of the country was prosperous and industrialised. The south was desperately poor. One statesman summed up the problem of Italy in this way: 'Italy is made. Now we must make Italians'.

2   The Unification of Germany

For many hundreds of years Germany, like Italy, was divided up into small states. There were over three hundred of them, each with their own rulers and governments. Some of them were not much bigger than a good-sized field. Others were large states with famous kings and powerful armies.

In the nineteenth century all of these states were slowly abolished. Germany became a unified country ruled by a single government. How did such a great change come about?

Napoleon and Germany

The story of German unity began with Napoleon Bonaparte. You will remember that while he was Emperor of France, Napoleon conquered most of Germany. When he had done this he did away with most of the small states. In their place he set up about thirty states, whose rulers were loyal to him. He called these states the Confederation of the Rhine, and encouraged their rulers to introduce reforms in their government.

Many Germans were annoyed at these conquests. They claimed that a French emperor had no right to interfere in the affairs of Germany. Some of these people such as Johann Fichte, wanted the German people to unite and drive Napoleon out of Germany. They pointed out that all Germans spoke the same language and were part of a single nation. Therefore, they argued that Germany should be united, free and independent.

Austria and Germany

One person who disagreed with these ideas was Prince von Metternich, the Chief Minister of Austria. We saw earlier that Metternich opposed Italian unity because he knew that it would weaken the Austrian Empire. He opposed the idea of German unity for the same reason. He knew that if Germany was united she would be a powerful nation—far more powerful than Austria. Therefore in 1815, after Napoleon had been defeated, Metternich made sure that Germany remained divided up into small states.

Despite this, many Germans still looked forward to the day when their country would be united. Some of them joined patriotic clubs and societies. There, over a glass of beer or a cup of coffee, they discussed plans for uniting their country. Other nationalists wrote books and pamphlets on the subject. In 1841 Hoffman von Fallersleben wrote a song in praise of Germany. The song was called *Deutschland, Deutschland, über alles.* (Germany, Germany, above all other countries). Today that song is the national anthem of Germany.

Johann Gottlieb Fichte (1762–1814). A German philosopher, Fichte resented Napoleon's domination of Germany and French domination of Europe.

73

Fighting around a street barricade in Berlin in 1848.

The Revolts of 1848–49

In 1848 it seemed that the time for action had at last come. In that year there was a food shortage in all the states of Germany and people rioted against their governments. Many governments took fright at this rioting, and went into hiding. Metternich even left Austria and fled abroad to London. The German nationalists seized their chance. They held a meeting in Frankfurt and tried to hammer out a plan for uniting their country.

However, they talked far too much and did far too little. While they spent their time talking and discussing, the riots began to die down. By the spring of 1849 all the old governments were back in control of their states. All hope of uniting Germany had gone. Quietly the nationalists in Frankfurt packed their bags and went home. They had missed their chance.

A street barricade during the rioting in Vienna in 1848.

A debate in the Frankfurt Parliament 1848–9.

Otto von Bismarck (1815–98). He became chief minister of Prussia in 1862 and, after the final unification of Germany in 1871, was made Imperial Chancellor. He remained in power until, after a disagreement with Emperor William II, he was forced to resign in 1890. For almost thirty years Bismarck was not only the most powerful person in Germany, but also the most influential statesman in Europe.

Otto von Bismarck

After the failure of 1848–49, most nationalists in Germany were disappointed. They thought that Germany could never be united. However, in 1862 a remarkable man came to power in the state of Prussia. That man was Otto von Bismarck, and he changed the course of German history.

Bismarck was a huge man with large staring eyes and broad shoulders. Most people who met him thought that he was a charming person. They said that he was polite and interesting to talk to. He was also an extremely clever politician who knew how to get what he wanted. His main ambition in life was to make Prussia into the most powerful state in Germany. In order to do this he was prepared to do anything. He was even prepared to go to war. He once said that Germany's problems would be solved only by 'blood and iron'. By this he meant the blood of defeated armies and the iron of Germany's industrial strength.

Prussia defeats Austria

Bismarck first planned to go to war with Austria. He was determined to stop Austria interfering in German affairs. So he laid careful plans. First he made sure that the Prussian armies were well trained and well equipped. He then persuaded the Italian government to support him with their armies. Finally in June 1866, when everything was ready, he declared war.

Everybody thought that Bismarck was foolish. They were sure that Prussia would be defeated. But they were wrong. On 3 July 1866 the Prussian armies defeated the Austrians in the Battle of Sadowa. The Austrian government quickly made peace and agreed to stop interfering in German affairs. This was exactly what Bismarck wanted, for it gave him the chance to increase the power of Prussia. In 1867 he did this by setting up the North German Federation. This brought all the states of northern Germany under the control of Prussia.

Bismarck and Southern Germany

Bismarck now turned his attention to the states of southern Germany: Bavaria, Württemburg and Baden. These states were still independent. How could Bismarck bring them under Prussian control? He decided that the best way of doing it was by war. If he could provoke another country to attack Prussia, then the three southern states would come to Prussia's assistance. Once they did this, he thought, they would agree to unite with Prussia. In this way the whole of Germany would be united.

The Franco-Prussian War

Bismarck soon saw a chance of bringing about a war. In 1869 Queen Isabella

76

The Battle of Sadowa (1866).

of Spain went into exile, leaving the throne of Spain vacant. The Spanish people immediately looked around for a new king, and some of them wanted to choose a German, Prince Leopold. This alarmed the French government, for Prince Leopold was a relative of the King of Prussia. The French were afraid that Prussia would become far too powerful if Leopold became King of Spain. So they asked their ambassador in Berlin to seek a meeting with the King of Prussia. They told him to ask the king to make sure that Leopold would not be King of Spain.

The French ambassador had a meeting with the king in the small German town of Ems. The king readily agreed to do as the French government asked. He did not want war with France. He then sent a telegram to Bismarck telling him what he had done.

When Bismarck received this telegram from Ems he was furious with the king. He wanted war with France so that he could unite Germany. So he did a very dishonest thing. He altered the wording of the Ems telegram to make it seem that the King of Prussia had insulted the French ambassador. He then told the newspapers to publish it. As he expected, the French were annoyed and immediately declared war on Prussia.

Germany defeats France

War broke out in July 1870. Within six months it was all over. The Prussian

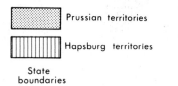

Prussian territories

Hapsburg territories

State
boundaries

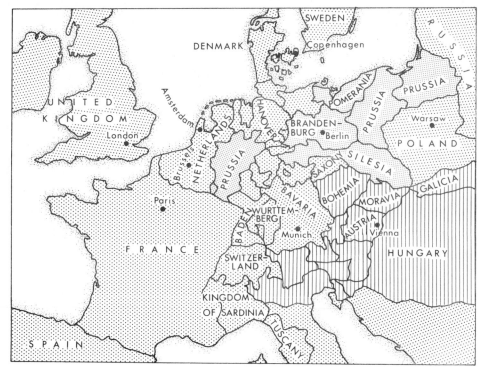

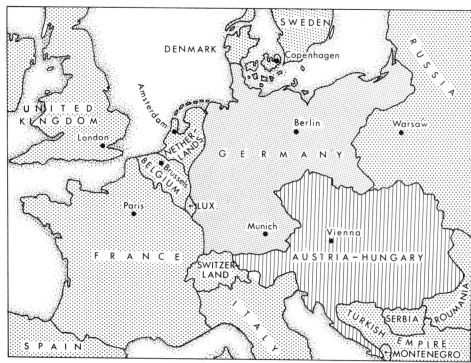

Germany after unification.

78

The French army surrenders at Metz in October 1870, after a short siege of the town.

armies were extremely powerful, well-equipped and fast. They forced the two main French armies to surrender at Sedan and Metz in October and November. Then, in January 1871, they marched into Paris. France had no option but to surrender.

Meanwhile, during the war, the three southern states of Germany joined Prussia in the fight against France. When the war was over they decided to give up their independence to join a united Germany. This was exactly what Bismarck had hoped for, and he managed to persuade the three states to accept the King of Prussia as the Emperor of the new Germany. On 18 January 1871, in the splendid Hall of Mirrors at Versailles the new emperor was crowned. King William I of Prussia became Emperor William I of Germany. The unification of Germany was complete.

The new Germany was the most powerful country in Europe. She had a population of over forty million people. She also had powerful armies and efficient industries. Bismarck's policy of 'blood and iron' had certainly succeeded.

TO DO

1   Use your textbook on medieval history to find out all you can about famous Italians in the Middle Ages. See especially if you can find out something about Dante, Michelangelo and Machiavelli.

King William I of Prussia (1797–1888).

2 Use an encyclopedia to find out more about Cavour, Garibaldi and Mazzini.

3 You are a newspaper reporter and you have an interview with Bismarck in 1871, after the unification of Germany. Tell your readers what sort of a mood Bismarck was in, what sort of a person he was, and what he did for Germany.

TO READ

Bismarck and the Unification of Germany, Archive Series, A. R. C. Hewison, Arnold.
Bismarck, the Kaiser and Germany, B. J. Elliott, Longman Group.
The Siege of Paris and the Commune, Jackdaw Series no. 59, Jackdaw Publications.
Garibaldi and the Risorgimento, Jackdaw Series no. 74, Jackdaw Publications.

DATELINE

1831	Mazzini exiled from Italy.
1834	Garibaldi exiled from Italy.
1841	German national anthem composed.
1848–9	Revolutions in Italy and Germany both end in failure.
1852	Cavour comes to power in Piedmont.
1859	Battle of Villafranca.
1862	Bismarck comes to power in Prussia.
1866	Battle of Sadowa.
1870	The Franco-Prussian War.
1871	King William I of Prussia becomes Emperor of Germany.

The German armies march into Paris.

5   Changes in the Economy, 1760–1870

During the nineteenth century great changes were made in the way that people lived and worked. New methods of farming were introduced. Factories were built. Railways and canals were constructed. Many clever men invented new machines which speeded up industrial production.

In this chapter you will see how all these changes came about. You will read about the inventors and the machines that they invented.

A harvest scene before new methods of farming were introduced.

1 The Agricultural Revolution

Men and women cannot live unless they have food. They need food in order to give energy and strength to their bodies. Because of this farming is one of the oldest occupations of the human race. Most of the people that have ever lived on this planet have been farmers.

The Old Style of Farming

For many thousands of years farmers were very wasteful and inefficient. They rarely had whole fields of their own. Instead they had strips of land in huge open fields. This meant that they had to grow the same crops as their neighbours. The ploughs that they used were made of wood and were dragged along by slow heavy oxen. This meant that ploughing the land was slow and difficult. Worst of all, farmers had to leave their land uncultivated once every four years, so that it could recover its richness for growing more crops. This year of rest was called the fallow year.

From 1760 onwards many changes began to take place. These changes improved agriculture so much that they have been called the Agricultural Revolution. Let us take a look at what this agricultural revolution was. We will look at it in England. For it was in England that the changes first took place.

Enclosures

One of the most important changes was the enclosure of land. This was done in many different ways. Sometimes waste land was enclosed. This meant that land which had never been used before was fenced round and used as farm land. It was then used for growing crops or grazing cattle.

Sometimes the open fields in a village were enclosed. When this happened the farmers who owned the individual strips of land in that field gave them up in return for a single block of land. They could then put a fence around that block of land, and farm it in whatever way they wanted.

Sometimes the common land in the village was enclosed. Common land was usually used by all the farmers in the village. So when it was enclosed all the farmers received a share of it. They could then go ahead and farm it as they wanted to.

Between 1750 and 1850 over six million acres of land in England were enclosed. Much waste land was farmed for the first time, and many open fields were divided up into individual farms.

Who benefited from all this enclosure? Undoubtedly the rich farmers did. They could afford to spend money on improving waste land. They also owned many of the strips in the open fields and so received large shares of

the field when it was divided up. For the same reason they usually took the biggest share of the common land. On the other hand the small farmer only received small shares of the land from the open fields and common land. Often these shares were too small for him to farm economically—so he was forced out of business. Many small farmers sold their land and became labourers, working for rich farmers. Others packed up their belongings and went to the nearest town in search of work. The days of the small farmer were numbered.

New Crop Rotations

Once a farmer had enclosed land he was able to experiment with new crops. Until the eighteenth century all farmers left their land fallow every four years. However, in the eighteenth century some of them began to try out new crops such as turnips, swedes, or clover. They soon discovered that if they used these crops in rotation with their normal crops, they never had to leave the land fallow. This was because turnips, swedes and clover produced special chemicals which gave life to the soil.

Farmers soon realised how useful these new crops were. Firstly they could use their land every year, instead of three years in every four. Secondly they

A special horse-hoe, invented by Jethro Tull in the early eighteenth century, which speeded up the task of ploughing.

could feed their cattle turnips and swedes throughout the cold winter months. This meant that they no longer had to slaughter their cattle every autumn. Instead they could keep them alive. As a result the farmer could save money, and the housewife could buy fresh meat throughout the winter.

'Turnip' Townshend

One person who encouraged the farmers to use the new crops was Viscount Charles Townshend. Townshend started off life as a politician. But one day he had a quarrel with the Prime Minister. He became so angry that he gave up politics and retired to his large farms in Norfolk. There he began to use a special crop rotation known as the Norfolk four-course rotation. As you can see from the diagram on this page, this involved using turnips every four years. Because of this the local people soon called him 'Turnip' Townshend. He did not mind this name because he was proud of the fact that he used turnips. Soon he taught other farmers to use them also. In this way he helped to improve the standard of farming.

(i) *Norfolk four-course crop rotation*

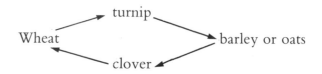

Jethro Tull (1674–1741).

New Machines on the Farm

These new crops made it important for farmers to have good machinery. Many new types of machines were invented. One of the most famous was the seed drill invented by Jethro Tull in 1701. This was a machine which planted seeds mechanically, and did away with the wasteful method of planting seed by hand. It was certainly a clever invention, but it was so

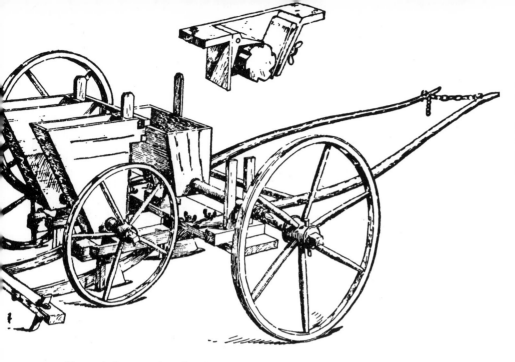

The seed drill, invented by Jethro Tull, planted seeds mechanically. The seeds were put into the two boxes at the back. As the wheels went round they moved the cog (inset) and the seeds were released into the drills.

complicated that it often broke down. As a result very few farmers ever used it.

Another invention was the threshing machine. This was invented by a Scotsman, Andrew Meikle, in 1786. It speeded up the work of harvesting corn crops. New ploughs were also designed. They were made of iron instead of wood, so that they lasted longer. Some of them were made so that they went deep down into the soil, and so ploughed a better furrow.

The light Rotherham plough was introduced in 1730.

BARRETT, EXALL, AND ANDREWES'
PATENT FOUR HORSE THRASHING MACHINE WITH PATENT GEAR WORK,
AS IN OPERATION.

Although this picture of a man standing beside a Lincolnshire ox may be exaggerated, it does show that cattle became bigger than they had been before.

Opposite (top)
The Norfolk plough in use about 1770.

Opposite (bottom)
An early threshing machine. There are places for four horses, although only two are working. Why, do you think, has the boy a whip?

Robert Bakewell and Cattle

Many farmers also wanted to have heavier and stronger cattle. Therefore they experimented with new breeds. One person who was successful at this was Robert Bakewell, a farmer from Leicestershire. He bred a new type of sheep called the New Leicester. This was heavier and meatier than other sheep. Other farmers followed his example, and soon most types of cattle were bigger than ever before. This meant that farmers got more money when they sold their cattle. It also meant that there was more meat in the shops for people to buy.

Robert Bakewell (1725–95).

Robert Bakewell's New Leicester sheep commonly called a 'Two-Pounder'. Of it Bakewell said that England 'had two pounds of mutton where there was only one before'.

87

1710	370 lbs	1710	50lbs	1710	38 lbs
1795	800 lbs	1795	150 lbs	1795	80 lbs
	Oxen		Calves		Sheep

A GOOD NAME IS RATHER TO BE CHOSEN THAN GREAT RICHES PROV. CH. 22. V. 1.

The North Erpingham
AGRICULTURAL ASSOCIATION.
(ESTABLISHED 1834.)
For the encouragement and Benefit of Industrious and deserving Cottagers
and Servants.

POSITIVELY THE LAST WEEK !!

People flocked to see the 'wonderfully large pig' of this advertisement.

J. MARSH,

HAS PURCHASED A

GREAT NOVELTY !!

Which may be SEEN ALIVE !!

AT THE

STAR YARD, OXFORD,

A WONDERFULLY

LARGE PIG,

Weighing 68 Score 12 lbs.,

From the Birmingham Cattle Show, Bred and Exhibited by W. B. WAINMAN, Esq., Yorkshire.

This is the Largest Pig ever seen and has gained 14 Prizes.

Admission, 2d., Children & Schools, 1d.

The PIG will be on her legs at 12, 2, 4, and 6 o'clock.

Hall and Son, Printers, New Road, Oxford.

Opposite (bottom)
How, do you think, does this scene show the influence of the Agricultural Revolution?

All the improvements that we have looked at in this chapter were first made in England. Only slowly did the farmers in the rest of Europe begin to use them as well. However, when they did, they soon found that they could produce more food than ever before. As a result the Agricultural Revolution brought the chance of a better life for everybody.

2   The Population Explosion

There are more people alive in the world today than ever before in the history of the human race. Tomorrow there will be even more. The population of the world is growing bigger and bigger every day. It looks as if it will go on growing for a long time to come. Some people call this the population explosion.

When did the population explosion start? Why did it happen? To answer these questions we have to go back two hundred years in time. This is because the population of Europe began to grow in about 1760. It has never stopped growing since.

Population Growth in Europe

How much did the population of Europe grow? Well, in 1760 there were about one hundred and fifty million people living in Europe. By 1870 there were almost three hundred million. So, as you can see, the population of Europe doubled in just one hundred and twenty years.

Let us now take a look at the main countries of Europe to see how their population grew. As you can see, most countries increased their population —some at a greater rate than others.

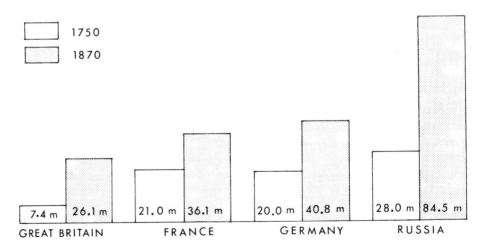

Populations, 1750–1870.

Let us now take a look at some of the cities and towns of Europe. You will see that their population also increased.

Legend: □ 1800   ▨ 1880

Values shown on bars: 172,000 1,122,000 1,117,000 4,770,000 547,000 2,269,000 82,000 553,000 250,000 612,000 247,000 726,000

BERLIN   LONDON   PARIS   LIVERPOOL   MOSCOW   VIENNA

Populations of some cities and towns of Europe, 1800–1880.

Why did the population of Europe suddenly start to grow in this way?

Better Food Supplies

One reason was that fewer people died of hunger than ever before. During the Middle Ages there were terrible famines when many people died of starvation. In the eighteenth century there were very few famines. In the nineteenth century there were even fewer, except for the terrible famine in Ireland in 1846.

Why were there so few famines in the eighteenth and nineteenth centuries? The answer is really quite simple. There were few famines because there was much more food in the shops for people to buy. Even when there were bad harvests there was usually enough food to go round. This was because the Agricultural Revolution, that we saw in the earlier part of this chapter, made it possible for farmers to produce more food than ever before. Better farming brought a better life for everybody.

Doctors and Disease

Another reason for the population growth was that doctors began to find out more about diseases. Nowadays, if we fall ill, we call the doctor. We know that he can cure us. However, doctors have not always been so clever and so

Edward Jenner (1749–1823) discovered a way of preventing smallpox.

reliable. For many hundreds of years doctors were really quite dangerous people. They did not know how the body worked. They knew nothing about such things as germs or bacteria. They just used old-fashioned ways of curing illnesses. More often than not these 'cures' made the patient more ill than ever before. One of the favourite medicines in the Middle Ages was made from cow manure. Cow manure certainly makes the grass grow, but it is not good for the human body.

Edward Jenner and Smallpox

However, some doctors in the eighteenth century did try to find out new ways of curing people. One such doctor was Edward Jenner. He discovered a way of preventing smallpox.

In Jenner's day smallpox was a terrible disease. Most people caught it, usually in their childhood. Many of them died from it. Others survived, but they were left with terrible scars on their face and body.

Jenner decided to try to stop this terrible disease. He was a doctor in the west of England and often had patients who caught smallpox. Whenever he treated these patients he was puzzled by one thing. All the local dairymaids caught the very mild disease of cowpox. They caught this from the cows that they milked. Yet they never caught smallpox. Did this mean that people who had caught cowpox were somehow protected against smallpox?

This cartoon shows Jenner and his friends driving off the quacks who did not wish to see vaccination against smallpox become popular because this would reduce their earnings.

VACCINATION against SMALL POX, Mercenary & Merciless spreaders of Death & Devastation driven out of Society

92

A small boy is amused by a puppet while he is being vaccinated.

Jenner decided to try to find out. In the spring of 1798 he deliberately infected a small boy, James Phipps, with cowpox. A few weeks later, when the boy had recovered, he tried to infect him with smallpox. However, as Jenner expected, the boy did not catch smallpox. He was protected against it. As doctors would say, he was immune to it.

Jenner's discovery was extremely important. It meant that doctors could inject small children with a mild dose of cowpox. The children would then never catch smallpox. Soon doctors all over Europe used Jenner's discovery, and smallpox became a very rare disease indeed.

Better food and better medicine therefore made a great difference to the people of Europe. People became much healthier and lived much longer than ever before. This was what started the population explosion.

Before the use of anaesthetics, operations, such as this one in the eighteenth century, were most painful and often resulted in the death of the patient.

The use of ether as an anaesthetic was first demonstrated in October 1846.

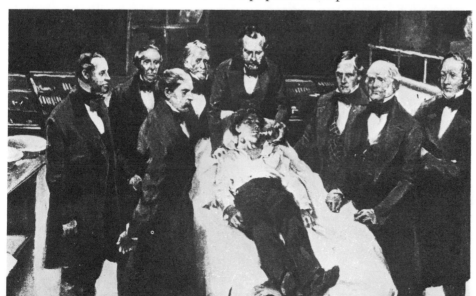

93

3   The Industrial Revolution

You saw in the first part of this chapter the great changes that were made in agriculture between 1760 and 1870. Now it is time to see the changes that were made in industry during the same period. New machines were invented which did the work of many men. They completely changed the way in which textiles, iron and coal were produced. These changes were so important that they have been called the Industrial Revolution. Let us take a close look at the inventions which caused the Industrial Revolution.

The Making of Cloth

In the eighteenth century the cloth industry was one of the biggest industries in Europe. Most of the cloth was made by people working in their own homes. Merchants from the local towns came round one week and supplied them with the raw material. The next week, they came round to collect the finished cloth. People liked this way of working because they could work at their own speed. They also liked it because they could do some farming as well, and so make their living from two jobs. Because people were able to work at home it was called the 'domestic system'.

A family spins and reels yarn.

James Hargreaves invented a spinning machine in 1765. He called it a 'spinning jenny' after his wife Jenny.

All the work that went into making the cloth was done by hand. There were two main jobs involved. The first was spinning, which made a long yarn out of the raw wool or cotton. This was done on a spinning wheel. The second was weaving, which weaved the yarn into a finished cloth. This was done on a loom. Spinning was usually done by women or girls, as it was a light task. Weaving was done by men, as the looms were heavy and difficult to work.

The Spinning Jenny

During the eighteenth century many people began to notice that spinning was a much slower job than weaving. The weavers often ran out of yarn and had to wait for the spinners to produce more. Several people therefore tried to invent machines that would increase the speed of spinning. The first successful machine was invented by an Englishman, James Hargreaves, in 1765. He called it the 'spinning jenny', after his wife, Jenny Hargreaves. The spinning jenny could be worked by one man, and it spun eight yarns all at the same time.

The Water Frame and the Mule
In 1768 another Englishman, Sir Richard Arkwright, made an even faster machine. This was called a water frame because it was powered by water. It could spin hundreds of yarns. However, the yarns that it produced were

Richard Arkwright (1732–92).

Arkwright's improved spinning machine or water-frame.

Samuel Crompton (1753–1827).

Crompton's 'mule'.

Mule spinning in a factory.

97

Power-loom weaving in a factory.

rather thick. They were not very good for the finer cloths. So in 1779 a man called Samuel Crompton invented a better machine. It could spin hundreds of yarns (like the water frame), but it also made very fine ones (like the spinning jenny). So, because it was a cross between the water frame and the spinning jenny, Crompton called his invention the 'mule'.

The Power Loom

These three machines speeded up the work of spinning. Now the spinners made so much yarn that the weavers could not use it all up. What the weavers needed was a machine to speed up the work of weaving. This machine was invented by a clergyman, Edmund Cartwright, in 1785. He made a 'power loom', which was driven by a steam engine. It could weave cloth much faster than any hand worker. At first the power loom was unreliable and often broke down. However, soon all the problems were solved. By 1850 almost all weaving was done on this new machine.

The Rise of Factories

These inventions brought about many changes in the way that spinners and weavers lived and worked. In the first place the new machines were mostly used for making cotton cloth, rather than woollen cloth. This was because

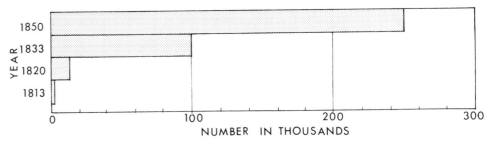

Number of power looms in Britain.

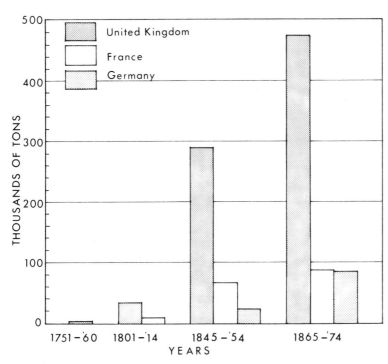

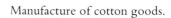
Manufacture of cotton goods.

the machines were quite rough and often broke the woollen yarn. Cotton was tougher, and much more easy to use. So cotton became a much more popular material than wool.

Secondly all the new machines were big and expensive. Because of this their owners put them into large sheds, that were soon known as factories. So instead of working at home, people had to go and work in factories. This was a great hardship. It meant that people had to work regular hours instead of working at their own pace. It also meant that they had to move their home so that they could live near the factory. As a result, the 'domestic system' soon began to die out.

Changes in the Iron Industry

While all these changes were taking place in the textile industry, there were also changes taking place in the iron industry. People invented new ways of making iron so that it became plentiful and cheap.

There were two main processes in the making of iron. During the eighteenth century inventors found ways of making them both faster and more efficient.

Abraham Darby

The first stage in iron making was to change the iron ore (which was dug

Edmund Cartwright (1743–1823).

99

Output of pig iron.

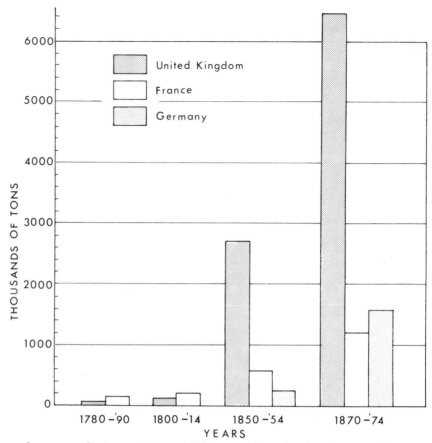

from the ground), into pig iron. This was done by heating up the iron ore over a charcoal fire until it became molten. The impurities then floated to the surface and were scraped off. The iron that was left was then allowed to cool down and it was called pig iron. All this was very slow and expensive. As a result people began to look for a cheaper way of making pig iron. In 1709 an ironmaster, Abraham Darby, showed that coke could be used instead of charcoal in order to heat the iron. Coke was made from coal. It was cheaper and much more plentiful than charcoal. Therefore Abraham Darby's invention meant that pig iron could be made more cheaply than ever before.

Puddling and Rolling

Pig iron was used to make certain things. However, it was very brittle. So in order to make it tougher it was heated up again, and the impurities were knocked out of it with hammers. This made the pig iron into wrought iron. Wrought iron was tough and could be used to make machines, tools, pots and pans. However, the task of hammering out the impurities was slow and

Pig iron being heated for 'puddling'.

In 'rolling' the iron, still hot, is passed through rollers.

Bending the iron tyre for a railway carriage wheel.

A Bessemer steel plant in operation. Molten pig iron was poured into the 'converters' (on left and right), a blast of air was blown in through the bottom and this burned off the impurities, mainly carbon. The purified iron was poured from the converter into a ladle (on the right).

expensive. So in 1784 a man called Henry Cort invented a new way of making iron into wrought iron. He called it 'puddling and rolling'. First the pig iron was heated up and stirred. This was called 'puddling', and got rid of the impurities. Then while it was still hot, the iron was squeezed through rollers. This was called 'rolling', and it made the iron into slabs of wrought iron. Puddling and rolling was a cheap way of producing good iron. It was also a very efficient way.

These new inventions made a great difference to the iron industry. Iron was now cheaper than ever before. Soon people began to use it for making new machines. They used it (as we saw earlier) to make ploughs. They used it (as we shall see shortly) to make railways.

However, before iron could be used for all these things, there was still one problem that had to be solved. That was the problem of how to get more coal in order to make greater amounts of pig iron.

The Problems of Coal Mining
In the eighteenth century there were many coalmines in Europe. However, the mine shafts never went very deep underground. This was because after a certain depth the shaft was always flooded with water. What the coalminers wanted to do was to get the water out of the shaft, in order to dig deeper and mine for better coal.

In the 1850s Henry Bessemer developed a method of making 'mild' steel by passing a blast of air through molten pig iron. This was a quicker and cheaper way of making steel.

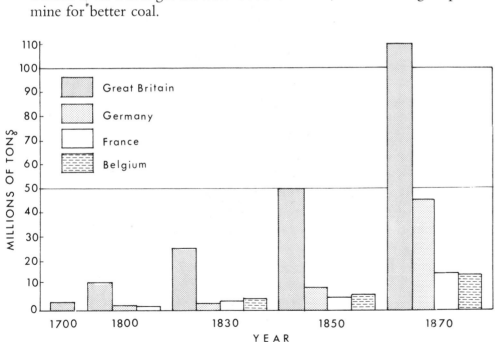

Output of coal.

103

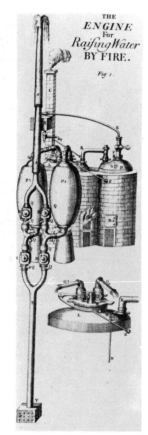

Thomas Savery invented the 'engine for raising water by fire' (a double pump) in 1698.

The Invention of the Steam Engine

Many people tried to invent ways of getting the water out of the mine shafts. One person even used five hundred horses to hoist up the water in buckets! However, in 1698 an Englishman, Thomas Savery, came up with the answer. He invented a mechanical pump which pumped the water out of the shaft. This pump was driven by steam, and soon came to be known as a 'steam engine'.

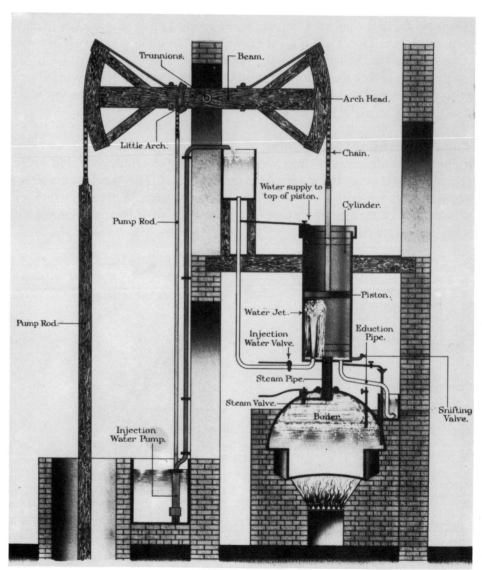

A diagram of Thomas Newcomen's pumping engine.

In 1705 another Englishman, Thomas Newcomen, made a more efficient steam engine. This could be used in very deep mines. Then, in 1775, a Scottish engineer called James Watt, invented an even better engine. It was more powerful and much more economical than Newcomen's. It was also better designed, and could pump water out of the deepest shafts. As a result, mines could go further underground than ever before, without any risk of flooding. This made coalmines more efficient and increased the amount of coal produced.

All these inventions made great changes in the industries of Europe. More goods were produced than ever before, as machines speeded up the process of production. This brought great wealth to the factory owners. But, as we shall see, it brought great misery and unhappiness to the factory workers.

A Newcomen winding engine (left) in operation at a coal pit-head. The machine on the right is for weighing coal.

Travelling in a crowded coach, on uneven roads, could be very uncomfortable.

4   The Transport Revolution

In the eighteenth century there were no fast methods of transport. The quickest way for a person to travel was on horseback. The best way of moving heavy goods was by sailing ship. There were no cars, no aeroplanes and no spaceships.

However, between 1760 and 1870 many improvements in transport began to take place. Roads were improved and canals were built. The railway was invented and the old sailing ships were gradually replaced by steamships. These improvements were so important that they have been called the Transport Revolution.

The Building of Better Roads
Let us start with the improvements in roads. In the eighteenth century most roads in Europe were very bad. In the winter they were muddy and full of dangerous potholes. In the summer they were so hard that they broke the wheels of the stagecoaches. What was needed was a smooth and well-drained type of road, which could be used safely all the year round.

Thomas Telford
Towards the end of the eighteenth century some roadbuilders began to build

A broken wheel could cause a serious accident.

such roads. The most famous of these roadbuilders was Thomas Telford. He was the son of a Scottish shepherd, but spent most of his life planning and building roads in various parts of Britain.

Telford believed that roads needed to have a firm foundation of heavy stones. This, he thought, would make the road strong, and also allow the rain water to drain away. He then believed that a layer of small stones should be spread over this foundation, so that the road had a good surface. Using these methods Telford built almost one thousand miles of road. His most famous achievement was the London to Holyhead road which linked London with the ferry to Dublin. There had always been a road between London and Holyhead. However, it had become so bad that in 1815 parliament asked Telford to make it suitable for coach traffic. Telford did this between 1815 and 1826. He made the road as flat and as straight as possible. He also built a bridge between the mainland of Wales and Anglesey. This bridge is still in use today.

Thomas Telford (1757–1834).

Canal Fever

Even after men like Telford had improved the roads it was still very costly to transport heavy loads on them. Instead, people preferred to send their heavy loads by boat. However, the rivers were not always suitable for this. Sometimes they did not link up the right places. At other times they were too

A passenger boat on the Grand Canal.

shallow. Therefore, during the eighteenth century, people began to build canals as a more dependable form of transport.

The first canal to be built in the British Isles was the Newry canal in Ireland. This was built in 1741 to link the town of Newry with the sea. Not long afterwards the Grand Canal was built in Dublin. This was eventually to stretch right across Ireland as far as the Shannon.

In England the first canal was built in 1761 by the Duke of Bridgewater. It was built to carry coal from his estates in Worsley to the factories of Manchester, seven miles away. It was so successful that other canals were soon built. They were designed to link up the main industrial areas of the country. In this way such goods as coal, iron, bricks and food could be easily transported to where they were needed. Altogether four thousand miles of canal were built in Britian between 1760 and 1830. Many of the canals are still in use today.

The Rise of the Railway

The great age of canal building came to an end in the 1830s. This was because of the invention of a new means of transport—the railway.

We saw earlier that a Scottish engineer, James Watt, improved the design of the steam engine in 1775. A few years later, in 1782, Watt made another improvement. He linked the piston of the steam engine with a wheel, so that the steam engine drove the wheel around. This was an exciting invention. It meant that the steam engine could be used to drive wheeled vehicles. Soon many inventors were at work trying to design a vehicle that could be powered by a steam engine.

At first the inventors tried to make 'steam carriages', that would run on ordinary roads. However, they never really worked. Most of them were so

The Duke of Bridgewater who built the first canal in England, 1761.

108

JamesWatt (1736–1819).

Watt's rotative beam engine.

Steam carriages were noisy and heavy as shown in this artist's impression of what traffic would be like if they became popular.

Richard Trevithick (1771–1833).

A model of Trevithick's Penydarren locomotive, 1804.

In 1809 Trevithick demonstrated his *Catch-me-who-can* or passenger carrying railway at Euston Square, London.

110

noisy that people complained about them. Others were so heavy that they cracked the roads.

In 1804 a Cornish engineer called Richard Trevithick built a slightly different sort of machine. He made a 'steam locomotive' that ran along rails. He held a special exhibition run in South Wales to show how his machine worked. The locomotive chugged along ten miles of track, dragging behind it five coaches full of cheering passengers. The whole journey took five hours! Nevertheless, although it was dreadfully slow, the journey was a success. It showed that steam locomotives worked best when they ran on rails.

George Stephenson and the 'Rocket'

After this, many people started to build 'railway engines'. The most famous of them was George Stephenson, an engineer from Newcastle. He became interested in steam engines while he was still a young boy. He could repair an engine even before he could read or write! Soon he began to build his own steam locomotives. Between 1822 and 1825 he built a long stretch of railway between the town of Darlington and the port of Stockton. It was built to

The *Puffing Billy* locomotive (1813) at a colliery.

George Stephenson (1781–1848).

The opening of the Stockton and Darlington railway, 27 September 1825.

The advertisement for a locomotive which the Liverpool and Manchester railway inserted in the *Liverpool Mercury* of 1829.

take the coal from the coal mines of South Durham to Stockton, where it could be shipped to other parts of Britain. Many of the carriages on the line were drawn by horses. However, some were drawn by steam engines that Stephenson had built himself.

The Stockton-Darlington railway was a great success. Soon Stephenson was asked to build another railway line between Liverpool and Manchester. In 1829, when the line was nearly completed, a competition was held to find the best steam locomotive to work it. The competition took place on a

TO ENGINEERS AND IRON FOUNDERS.

THE DIRECTORS of the LIVERPOOL and MAN-CHESTER RAILWAY hereby offer a Premium of £500 (over and above the cost price) for a LOCOMOTIVE ENGINE, which shall be a decided improvement on any hitherto constructed, subject to certain stipulations and conditions, a copy of which may be had at the Railway Office, or will be forwarded, as may be directed, on application for the same, if by letter, post paid.

HENRY BOOTH, Treasurer.

Railway Office, Liverpool, April 25, 1829.

section of the track at Rainhill and was known as the Rainhill Trials. Many engineers entered their locomotives for the competition, but Stephenson won with the *Rocket*. It reached a speed of 35 m.p.h. In 1830 the Liverpool–Manchester railway was officially opened, with eight *Rockets* pulling the trains along it. It was the first railway line in the world to be run completely by steam locomotives.

The Liverpool–Manchester railway started the great 'railway age'. Soon many more railway lines were built to link up the big cities and towns of

Passenger carriage, 1870.

The remains of Stephenson's *Rocket*, 1829.

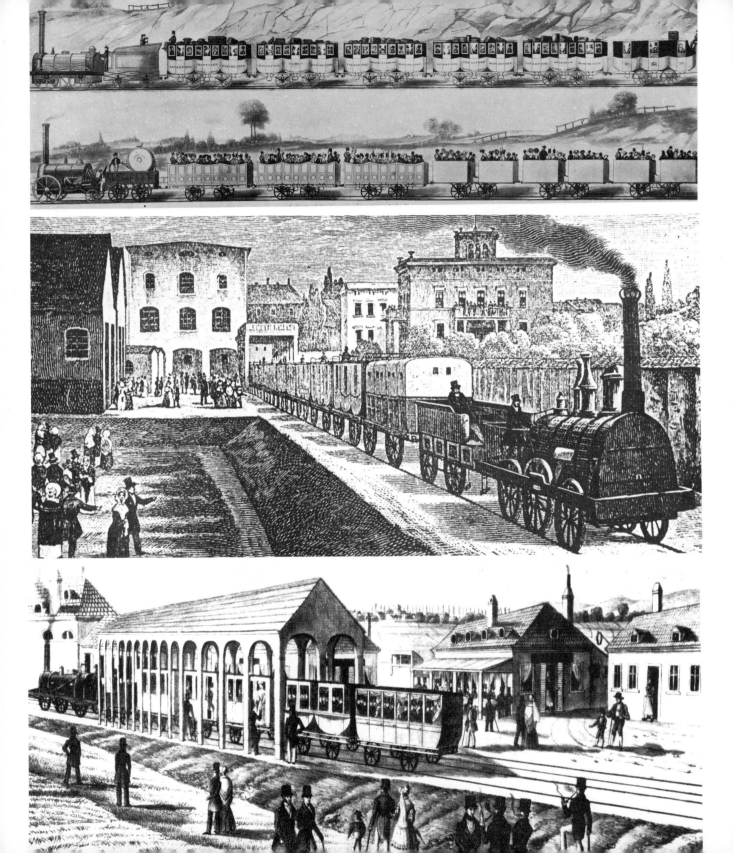

'The Cork Steamship Company's steamship *Sirius,* 700 tons, 320 horses power'.

Opposite (top)
Locomotive and first-class passenger carriages, 1831.
Locomotive and second-class passenger carriages, 1831.

Opposite (centre)
A train on the Berlin and Potsdam line, 1838.

Opposite (bottom)
An early Austrian train.

Britain. Elsewhere in Europe railways were also built. France, Ireland, Germany, Belgium, Russia and Italy had all begun to build railways before the end of the 1830s. By 1870 there were over sixty-five thousand miles of railway track in Europe.

The First Steamships

Engineers did not only use steam engines for railway locomotives. They also used them for ships. In 1816 the first sea-going steamship, the *Hibernia,* was launched. It sailed on the Holyhead-Dublin route. Soon larger ships were built that could travel greater distances. In 1838 two steamships crossed the Atlantic—the *Sirius* and the *Great Western.* This proved that the steamship could rival the old sailing ship.

The *Great Western* leaves Bristol for New York.

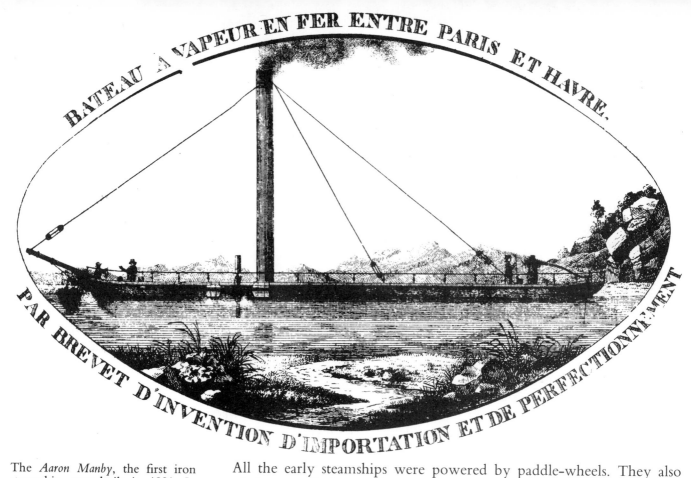

BATEAU À VAPEUR EN FER ENTRE PARIS ET HAVRE. PAR BREVET D'INVENTION D'IMPORTATION ET DE PERFECTIONNEMENT

The *Aaron Manby*, the first iron steamship, was built in 1821. In 1822 Aaron Manby built an iron steamship and travelled in it from London, across the English Channel and up the Seine to Paris.

All the early steamships were powered by paddle-wheels. They also carried some sails in case the engine broke down. Nevertheless they were fast and reliable. By 1870 people had stopped building sailing ships. Steamships ruled the waves.

These new inventions speeded up communications in Europe. People were able to travel around more quickly and more comfortably than ever before. Goods could also be moved around more easily and cheaply. As a result life became more enjoyable and industry was made more efficient.

TO DO

1 Find out more about the life and work of Edward Jenner.
2 Between 1760 and 1870 the population in Ireland did not grow as fast as in the rest of Europe. Why was this? Use your Irish history textbook for the nineteenth century to help you find the answer.
3 How did enclosures change the life of people who lived on the land?
4 Ask the farmers in your local area how they 'rotate' their crops in order to increase the yield from their land. Ask them how important fertilisers are in improving the quality of the soil.

Early German steamships, 1848–52.

5 Write an account of the life of one of the following people: 'Turnip' Townshend, Sir Richard Arkwright, James Watt, George Stephenson, Thomas Telford.
6 Make a date list of the various inventions in agriculture, industry and transport.
7 Find out more about the building of railways and canals in your own area.

TO READ

The Agrarian Revolution, Then and There Series, John Addy, Longman Group.
A Textile Community in the Industrial Revolution, Then and There Series, E. G. Power, Longman Group.
The Age of Factories, G. Middleton, Longman Group.
A Coal and Iron Community in the Industrial Revolution, Then and There Series, John Addy, Longman Group.
The Transport Revolution, Roger Watson, Longman Group.
Roads and Canals in the Eighteenth Century, Then and There Series, Marjorie Greenwood, Longman Group.
From Rocket to Railcar. An Outline of Rail Development since 1804, L. E. Snellgrove, Longman Group.
From Coracles to Cunarders, L. E. Snellgrove, Longman Group.
James Watt and Steam Power, Jackdaw Series no. 13, Jackdaw Publications.
The Great Exhibition, Jackdaw Series no. 43, Jackdaw Publications.

The *Great Eastern* steamship, 22,500 tons, built in 1858.

DATELINE

1698	Thomas Savery's steam engine.
1701	Jethro Tull's seed drill.
1705	Thomas Newcomen's steam engine.
1709	Abraham Darby first uses coke for the manufacture of iron.
1741	The building of the Newry Canal.
1761	The building of the Bridgewater Canal.
1765	James Hargreaves' spinning jenny.
1768	Richard Arkwright's water frame.
1775	James Watt's improved steam engine.
1779	Samuel Crompton's mule.
1784	Henry Cort invents 'puddling and rolling'.
1785	Edward Cartwright's power loom.
1786	Andrew Meikle's threshing machine.
1798	Edward Jenner discovers a cure for smallpox.
1804	Richard Trevithick tries out his steam locomotive.
1815–26	Telford builds the London-Holyhead road.
1822–25	The building of the Stockton-Darlington railway.
1829	The Rainhill Trials.
1830	The opening of the Liverpool-Manchester railway.
1838	The *Sirius* and the *Great Western* cross the Atlantic.

6 The Social Problems, 1760–1870

In the last chapter you read about the great economic changes in Europe during the nineteenth century. In this chapter you will see the terrible problems that these changes caused for working people. You will read about overcrowding and disease in towns. You will also read about bad housing, slums and terrible working conditions in factories. You will discover how trades unions started up, and you will read about the ideas of Karl Marx.

A time of overcrowding and disease in towns.

By 1870 more people lived in towns than ever before.

1   Disease and Overcrowding in Towns

We saw in the last chapter that the population of Europe doubled in size between 1760 and 1870. We also saw that the number of people who lived in towns increased at an even greater rate. By 1870 more people lived in towns than ever before in the whole history of the human race. This caused many problems.

In this chapter we will see what these problems were. We shall then see how governments tried to solve them.

Slums and Overcrowding

One of the problems that town dwellers faced in this period was the shortage of housing. The population of most towns grew so fast that there were not enough houses for everybody. Even when new houses were built they were very small and crowded together. They quickly became untidy slums.

As a result of the lack of housing, poor people in most towns had to rent rooms to live in. Often two families shared the same room, and took it in turns to use the bed. The rooms were usually damp, dark and filthy. In Liverpool in 1840 there were forty thousand people living in cellars. In many of these cellars eight people had to share the same bed. In Bristol over half the working-class families had only one room to their name. Living conditions were the same for the poor all over Europe. In Berlin in 1830 a government official found a family of seven sleeping together in a small bed, in a dark and damp room.

New houses, small and crowded together, quickly became slums.

121

All towns were smelly, dirty and unhealthy.

The number of infants dead at birth was very high. This midwife on her way to a birth would hardly inspire confidence.

A MIDWIFE GOING TO A LABOUR.

Dirt and Disease

Another problem in these towns was the lack of proper sanitation. All towns were smelly, dirty and unhealthy. The streets were usually narrow and dark. The pavements were usually covered with rubbish and sewage because there were no proper drains. This was dangerous for the poor pedestrian, as people often threw rubbish out of their windows onto passers-by. It was also very dangerous for people's health because the rubbish rotted on the pavement and helped to spread disease. Even the drinking water was dirty. It was usually taken straight from rivers, which were full of rubbish and dirt.

Men, women and children visited the gin-shop.

Disease spread quickly in these conditions. Some people died of chest diseases such as tuberculosis. Others died from typhus which was spread by the dirty drinking water. The worst disease of all was cholera. This had always been a common disease in India, but in 1831 it began to appear in Europe. Those who caught it suffered from terrible stomach pains and sickness, and died a slow and painful death. Cholera was a killer disease and it killed thousands.

Crime and Drunkenness
One further problem caused by the growth of towns was the problem of

Opium smoking.

A watchman makes his nightly round while, in the background, thieves break into a house.

crime. The poor people, who lived in these terrible conditions, led a miserable life. They had no hope of ever seeing better days. So, many of them turned to drink and drugs for comfort and relief. The working classes in France drank wine. The working classes in Germany and England drowned their sorrows in beer and gin. Some of them even turned to drugs and smoked opium.

However, many people did not only turn to drink. They also turned to crime. All over Europe the crime rate steadily grew. The poor people stole food that they could not afford to buy. They picked pockets in order to get

money to live. In Paris, almost sixty thousand people made their living from crime alone. Theft, murder and street fights were quite common in the poorer quarters of most towns.

During the nineteenth century many people worried over the problems and misery of town life. They worked hard to put them right, and also encouraged governments to take action. Two people who were most active in this way were Edwin Chadwick and Sir Robert Peel.

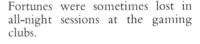

Fortunes were sometimes lost in all-night sessions at the gaming clubs.

The cockfight was a favourite pastime of all classes. Here money is being stolen from the blind aristocrat (centre) while (on the left) a deaf man uses his hearing-horn. Even a chimney-sweep (right) has taken time off to watch. The shadow (centre) is of a man who has been raised up in a basket for not paying his debt. He offers his watch as payment.

125

Some better-off people take afternoon tea at a tea-house.

Edwin Chadwick saw for himself the terrible conditions which existed in the towns.

126

A pedlar offers his rat-traps for sale.

Edwin Chadwick and Public Health

Edwin Chadwick was a hard-working government official in Britain. People thought him a grumpy bad-tempered person. However, he visited many cities and towns throughout Britain, and saw for himself the terrible conditions that existed in all of them. In 1842 he published a *Report on the Sanitary Conditions of the Labouring Classes*. In this report he showed that disease in towns was due to bad housing and bad sanitation. 'Disease' he said, 'is always found in connection with damp and filth, and close and overcrowded dwellings'.

Chadwick's report shocked many people. It made them realise that some-

A fishmonger and a milkmaid sell their goods. Do you think the fish and milk were clean?

thing had to be done to make towns more clean and healthy. So, in 1848, parliament passed the Public Health Act. This set up a General Board of Health to look after the problems of sanitation in Britain's towns. This board encouraged towns to set up their own health boards in order to supervise such things as sewage and street cleaning. Soon improvements were made in many towns. Sewers were built and running water was supplied to many houses. These improvements made towns much more healthy and many diseases began to disappear.

Florence Nightingale (1820-1910), seen here in a military hospital at Scutari, was shocked by the filthy conditions in which wounded soldiers were treated. In 1860 she founded a nurses' training school in London. Before this, nursing was regarded as an unskilled job. She was called 'the lady with the lamp' because she used go through the hospital wards last thing at night to make sure that everything was in order.

128

A public hanging. Two boys (on right) are more interested in picking a man's pocket.

Robert Peel (1788–1850).

Sir Robert Peel and the British Police

Sir Robert Peel tried to deal with the problem of crime in Britain. He was Home Secretary from 1822 until 1830. Peel saw that criminals were rarely punished for their crimes, because there was no effective police force in the country. He decided that if a police force was set up, most criminals would be discouraged from stealing. So, in 1829, he set up a police force of three thousand men for the city of London. They were all dressed in a special uniform with a top hat and a wooden truncheon. Because of Peel's own name they came to be known as 'peelers' or 'bobbies'. They soon caught many thieves and murderers in London. As a result the worst criminals left

the city, and went to other towns in Britain where there was no police force. So, in 1856, parliament passed a new Act. This made it necessary for all towns to set up their own police force. Soon the policeman was a familiar sight on the streets of Britain.

Reform of the Criminal Code

Peel also took steps to reform the criminal code. When he came to power in 1822 he found that there were over two hundred sorts of crime that carried the death penalty. He thought that this was cruel. He also noticed that it did not deter people from committing crimes. He began therefore to reduce the number of crimes punishable by death. By 1854 people could be executed only if they were found guilty of murder or high treason. The punishments for many other crimes were also reduced and made more humane.

The reforms of Edwin Chadwick and Sir Robert Peel helped to prevent disease and cut down crimes. However, they were only a start. There was still much to be done before city life could become safe and enjoyable.

2 Factory Work and Trade Unions

We saw in Chapter 5 that the Industrial Revolution brought about the rise of the 'factory system'. Men and women no longer worked at home. Instead they worked in factories.

These changes created many problems for the new 'working class' in the factories. In this section we shall see what those problems were. We shall also see the attempts that were made to put them right.

Long Hours of Work

One of the worst problems for the working class was the long hours that they had to work. Usually they had to start work in the factory at six in the morning. They never finished work until eight at night, and often they had to work much later. In fact most factory workers worked a fifteen-hour day, six days a week. At night people trudged home to snatch a few hours' sleep. Then when dawn came, they were up again and off to work. When Sunday came they were exhausted. All they could do was to rest in preparation for another week's work. There was no time for a chat around the fireside or a walk in the open air.

Dangers of Work

The conditions that people worked in were also terrible. In the coalmines many miners caught deadly lung diseases from breathing the coal dust. Others were crippled or killed by underground explosions and rock falls. In

130

the textile factories workers caught chest diseases and rheumatism because of the damp air. Others were injured by the huge spinning and weaving machines. Some workers were crushed to death and others lost an arm or a leg. Many workers suffered from spinal injuries because they had to bend and stoop over their machines. In one factory in France children were suspended from the ceiling by a long strap tied around their waist. This left their arms and legs free to operate the machinery, but it made many children suffer from injuries to their backs.

Low Wages
The wages for all this work were not very good. The factory owners always paid low wages so that they could make large profits for themselves. In some cases they forced the workers to spend their wages at special factory shops. These shops were run by the factory owners and charged very high prices for the food and clothing that they sold. As a result the workers got very little for their money and the factory owners gained a good profit. This was called the 'truck system'. It meant that the workers had to spend all their money and had no chance to save any of it. This meant that when they eventually lost their job, they had no savings to pay for their lodgings and food. They then had to beg or starve.

Women and Children in Factories
These conditions were bad enough for men. But we should remember that women and children suffered from them as well. Factory owners often preferred to employ women and children, because they could pay them lower wages then they paid to men. Sometimes children started to work in factories at the age of four, and worked for as many hours as their mothers and fathers did. Many of them died from overwork or from the diseases that they caught.

Women and children worked long hours in factories and even underground in the mines.

Opposite (top)
A 'peeler' or 'bobby'.

Opposite (bottom)
A young girl weary and dejected through long hours at work in a factory.

Setting a shot for blasting in a mine. Accidents often happened.

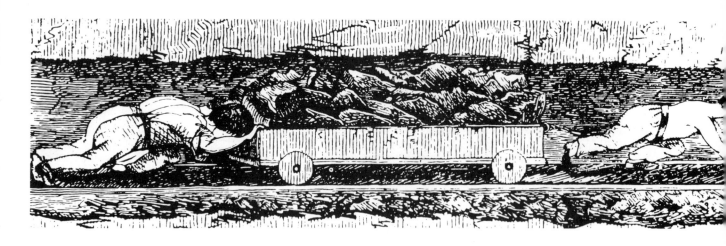

Obviously something had to be done to improve the conditions of the working class. But who could take any action? Certainly not the factory owners. They refused to improve the conditions of work and worried only about increasing their profits. It was left to governments, and to the workers themselves to take action. Governments passed laws to protect workers and to improve their conditions of work. Workers founded trades unions to fight for better wages.

Let us see how this was done in Britain. For it was in Britain that the Industrial Revolution, which caused all these problems, first happened.

Lord Shaftesbury and the Working Children

The British parliament passed many laws to improve the conditions of factory workers. Most of these laws were due to the work of a rich nobleman, Lord Shaftesbury. Shaftesbury was a deeply religious person. He believed that the duty of the rich was to help the poor. This made him anxious to improve the working conditions of factory workers, and especially those of the women and children. In 1842 he persuaded parliament to pass the Coal Mines Act. This made it illegal for women and children to work underground in the mines. In 1847 he persuaded parliament to pass the Ten Hours Bill, which made it illegal for women and children to work in factories for more than ten hours a day. Other laws also made it illegal for children under nine years of age to work in factories.

The work of people like Lord Shaftesbury helped to improve the conditions of work in factories. However, the workers also took action to help themselves. They wanted higher wages, and safer working conditions. Therefore they set up trade unions.

Lord Shaftesbury (1801–85).

ROBERT'S first interview with M.ᴿ STOPS.

Young Robert, could read, but he gabbled so fast;

And ran on with such speed, that all meaning he lost.

Till one Morning he met M.ʳ Stops, by the way,

Who advis'd him to listen to what he should say.

Then, entring the house, he a riddle repeated,

To shew, WITHOUT STOPS, how the ear may be cheated.

A page from a children's book *Punctuation personified; or pointing made easy.*

Members of the Matchmakers Union march to present a petition to parliament for better wages and working conditions.

The Growth of Trade Unions

In the early nineteenth century workers in many industries in Britian set up their own trade unions. The factory owners and the government did not like this. They were afraid that the workers would become too powerful. Therefore, in 1834, the government prosecuted six farm labourers who belonged to a branch of the Labourer's Union. The six men came from the village of Tolpuddle in Dorset. They were sentenced to transportation to Australia for seven years hard labour. Many people thought that this was a very unfair sentence, and they called the men the 'Tolpuddle Martyrs'. Workers held public meetings all over Britain, and signed petitions protesting against the sentence. In 1836 the government finally agreed to pardon the men and allow them return to England.

After this, many workers joined trade unions. They saw that if they united with their fellow workers they could force the factory owners to give them higher wages and better working conditions. By 1870 over one million workers in Britain were members of trade unions.

The passing of the Factory Acts and the formation of trade unions both brought great benefits to the working man. They protected him against the worst evils of factory work, and made sure that he received a decent living wage. Since 1870 more Factory Acts have been passed and trade unions have become larger and more effective. Both of these developments have improved the standard of life for many people.

Opposite
This picture shows canvassers bribing voters with presents and money.

134

3   The Chartists and Karl Marx

You have now read about the terrible conditions in which people lived and worked during the nineteenth century. You have also read about people such as Edwin Chadwick and Lord Shaftesbury, who tried to improve those conditions.

However, there were many people who believed that these improvements did not go far enough. They wanted much more important changes to be made. One group of people in Britain, called the 'Chartists', wanted parliament to pass a 'Charter' which would give the vote to the working man. Once working men had the vote, they thought, parliament would pass laws to help the poor.

A German thinker, Karl Marx, had a different idea. He said that the workers should rise up in revolt against the factory owners. Then they should take over government and run society in the interests of the poor and needy. This idea was called 'socialism' or 'communism'.

Let us take a closer look at the ideas of the Chartists and of Karl Marx.

In 1832 a Reform Bill was passed in England. This gave more MPs (Members of Parliament) to the towns. Before this most of those who sat in the House of Commons were landowners. Some towns with big populations had few MPs while some small country places had too many. The few voters in these places usually worked for the local landowner and he often told them how to vote. The Reform Bill meant that most of these 'rotten boroughs', as they were called, were done away with.

Opposite
Until 1872 voting was public. At this polling booth the mad and even the dying are brought along to vote.

137

William Lovett and the Charter

The story of the Chartists begins in London in 1836. In that year a group of working men founded the London Working Men's Association (L.W.M.A.). The aim of their association was to reform parliament and to give the vote to the working class. Once this was done, they thought that parliament would pass laws to help the poor.

The leader of the L.W.M.A. was a hard-working cabinet maker, William Lovett. In 1838 he drew up a Charter containing all the demands of the L.W.M.A. It was a long document, but contained six essential points:

1 The vote for all adult men.
2 Election by secret ballot.
3 Electoral districts of equal size.
4 Abolition of the need for M.P.s to be wealthy men.
5 M.P.s to be paid a salary.
6 A new parliament to be elected every year.

The National Petition

Lovett wanted the Charter to be presented to parliament. But first he organised a huge national petition in support of it, to be signed by every working man. All over Britain workers signed and supported the Charter. They attended huge open-air meetings, heard speeches and cheered the Chartist leaders. The factory workers in the north of England were especially enthusiastic. They hoped that if parliament were to be reformed, the worst evils of factory work would be abolished.

Parliament refuses the Charter

In July 1839 the petition and the Charter were presented to parliament. However, most M.P.s did not believe that the working class should have a say in the running of the country. Therefore, parliament turned down the petition by two hundred and thirty-five votes to forty-six.

The Chartist leaders were bitterly disappointed. But they continued their campaign. In 1842 they presented a second petition to parliament with more than three million signatures. Once again parliament turned the petition down. In 1848 a third petition was organised. This time so many people signed the petition that three coaches were needed to carry it to the Houses of Parliament. However, when M.P.s looked at the signatures, they saw that many of them were forgeries—such as 'Queen Victoria', 'Mr. Punch' and 'Pug-nose'. For the third time, parliament turned the petition down.

This third refusal finished the Chartist movement. Most of the leaders were too disappointed to carry on. They had failed to persuade parliament

The Six Points
OF THE
PEOPLE'S
CHARTER.

The six points of the 'People's Charter'.

1. A VOTE for every man twenty-one years of age, of sound mind, and not undergoing punishment for crime.

2. THE BALLOT.—To protect the elector in the exercise of his vote.

3. No PROPERTY QUALIFICATION for Members of Parliament —thus enabling the constituencies to return the man of their choice, be he rich or poor.

4. PAYMENT OF MEMBERS, thus enabling an honest trades- man, working man, or other person, to serve a constituency, when taken from his business to attend to the interests of the country.

5. EQUAL CONSTITUENCIES, securing the same amount of representation for the same number of electors, instead of allowing small constituencies to swamp the votes of large ones.

6. ANNUAL PARLIAMENTS, thus presenting the most effectual check to bribery and intimidation, since though a constituency might be bought once in seven years (even with the ballot), no purse could buy a constituency (under a system of universal suffrage) in each ensuing twelvemonth; and since members, when elected for a year only, would not be able to defy and betray their constituents as now.

Subjoined are the names of the gentlemen who embodied these principles into the document called the "People's Charter," at an influential meeting held at the British Coffee House, London, on the 7th of June, 1837:—

Daniel O'Connell, Esq., M.P.,	Mr. Henry Hetherington.
John Arthur Roebuck, Esq., M.P.	Mr. John Cleave.
John Temple Leader, Esq., M.P.	Mr. James Watson.
Charles Hindley, Esq. M.P.	Mr. Richard Moore.
Thomas Perronet Thompson, Esq., M.P.	Mr. William Lovett.
William Sharman Crawford, Esq., M.P.	Mr. Henry Vincent.

W. COLLINS, PRINTER, "WEEKLY TIMES" OFFICE, DUDLEY

This French picture of a Chartist meeting in 1848 shows the Chartists as revolutionaries.

Karl Marx (1818–83).

to grant the vote to the working class. Nevertheless, if you look again at the six points of the Charter, you will see that most of the Chartist demands have now been granted. So, in many ways the Charter was ahead of its time.

Karl Marx

Karl Marx had ideas that were very different to those of the Chartists. Yet, like them, he wanted to help the working class towards a better life.

Marx was a German Jew, born in the city of Triers in 1818. As a young man he read many books and studied at the universities of Bonn and Berlin. However, people in high places soon heard that young Karl Marx had strong views on the rights of the poor. In 1843 Marx was ordered to leave Germany. He went first to Paris and then to Brussels. Finally, in 1848, he moved to London, where he lived for the rest of his life.

Marx was an impressive looking man. He was big and broad, with a mass of tangled hair and a huge beard. He spent most of his time working in the library of the British Museum. There, surrounded by piles of dusty manuscripts, he wrote newspaper articles, pamphlets and books. Life was not easy for him. Often he did not earn enough money from his books to pay for his rent and food. However, he had a good friend in Friedrich Engels. Engels was the son of a wealthy factory owner, and was able to give Marx a good deal of money. This helped Marx to live and to write many of his books.

Marx and Socialism

What were Marx's ideas for helping the poor? They can be found in his main books, the *Communist Manifesto* (1848) and *Das Kapital* (3 vols. 1867, 1885, 1894). He believed that, throughout history, rich people had always controlled government. They used the powers of the government to make themselves wealthy at the expense of the poor. In the Middle Ages, the nobility had owned all the land and were the richest people in society. They had therefore controlled the government of their country through the feudal system. Since the Middle Ages, Marx said, trade and industry had grown enormously. As a result of this growth, the 'middle class' of traders and factory owners had become richer than the nobility. They now controlled the government in many countries.

However, Marx pointed out that the middle class had only become rich by exploiting the working class. They made workers work long hours in factories and paid them very low wages. In this way they made huge profits for themselves, while the workers lived in poverty and misery.

Friedrich Engels (1820–95).

Workers in a well-organised factory.

Workers' houses were built close to the factories.

Without property, without a job, the life of the 'dispossessed' was not easy.

The Rise of the Working Class

Marx therefore claimed that the working class would soon revolt against this exploitation. They would take over the factories and start a completely new form of society. In this society no one would own anything and no one would work for anyone else. Instead, everything would be held in common and everyone would work for the good of the whole community. If everybody worked as well as they could, Marx believed that no one would be poor, and no one would be unhappy. He once said: 'From each according to his capacity. To each according to his needs.'

Socialism spreads to Europe

Marx's ideas are often called 'socialism' or 'communism'. This is because Marx wanted to reorganise *society* and to create a new sort of *community*. Soon these ideas became very popular. Many people read Marx's books and became converted to the cause of socialism.

In 1864 Marx called socialists from many countries to a special meeting in London. There they organised the First International Workingmen's Association to co-ordinate the activity of socialists throughout Europe. Soon every European country had a socialist party.

TO DO

1 You are the mayor of a large industrial town in the middle of the nineteenth century. Write a letter to the government about the living conditions in your town. Suggest ways in which the government could improve conditions.

142

2   You are a factory worker in the middle of the nineteenth century. Write
    a diary about a typical week in your life. Don't forget to mention your
    family, your home, your friends and the sort of factory where you work.
3   Charles Dickens wrote many books which describe the life of poor
    people in nineteenth-century England. Two of the best are *David Copper-
    field* and *Oliver Twist*. Find a copy of one of these books and try to read it.
4   Find out about Lord Ashley and what he did to help working people.
5   Use an encyclopedia to find out more about Karl Marx, and then write
    the story of his life.

Charles Dickens (1812–1870) gives
a public reading from his works.

TO READ

Social Conditions in England 1760–1830, Isley Doncaster, Longman Group.
A Hundred Years of Medical Care, Then and There Series, A. Delgado, Long-
man Group.
Florence Nightingale, A. Delgado, Harrap.
Police and Prisons, Then and There Series, P. F. Speed, Longman Group.
Edwin Chadwick, Poor Law and Public Health, Then and There Series, Roger
Watson, Longman Group.
British Trade Unionism 1850–1914, Archive Series, L. W. Evans, Arnold.
A Night in Cold Harbour, M. Kennedy.
Shaftesbury and the Working Children, Jackdaw Series no. 7, Jackdaw Publica-
tions.
The Vote, Jackdaw Series no. 16, Jackdaw Publications.
The Early Trade Unions, Jackdaw Series no. 35, Jackdaw Publications.
Elizabeth Fry and Prison Reform, Jackdaw Series no. 63, Jackdaw Publications.
London Peelers and the British Police, Jackdaw Series no. 88, Jackdaw Publica-
tions.

DATELINE

1818   Birth of Karl Marx.
1829   Peel establishes the police force in London.
1831   Cholera first comes to Europe.
1834   The Tolpuddle Martyrs.
1836   The founding of the L.W.M.A.: beginning of the Chartist movement.
1839   The Charter first presented to parliament.
1842   Chadwick's *Report on the Sanitary Conditions of the Labouring Classes*.
1847   Shaftesbury's Ten Hour Bill.
1848   Karl Marx publishes the Communist Manifesto.
1864   First meeting of the International Workingmen's Association.

7 The Age of Prosperity and Power, 1870–1914

Between 1870 and 1914 Europe became more prosperous and more powerful than ever before. New machines were invented and new industries started up production. People had more leisure time and began to take an interest in entertainment and sport. At the same time many countries made great conquests in Africa and Asia. They then established overseas empires for themselves.

In this chapter you will see how all these things happened. You will read about motor cars and aeroplanes, soccer and boxing. You will also read about explorers who went into the jungles of darkest Africa. This was the age of prosperity and power.

People had more time for leisure by the end of the nineteenth century: a summer's day on the beach at Margate in England around 1900.

MARGATE SANDS. 2900 X

L.S.& P.C

For those who could not afford to get to the seaside, there was always the ragged organ-grinder with his performing monkey.

1 New Inventions and Discoveries

The years between 1870 and 1914 were full of interesting discoveries and inventions. Doctors discovered new medicines and new ways of curing illnesses. Engineers invented many different types of machines which made life

Louis Pasteur (1822–95). French chemist and biologist who discovered the cure for rabies and developed the use of antiseptics in surgery.

more exciting and more enjoyable. Many of the machines and gadgets that we use today were invented during this period.

Medical Discoveries

Let us first look at the discoveries made by doctors. Many of these discoveries made it possible for doctors to cure illnesses that had previously been considered to be fatal. A French doctor, Louis Pasteur, showed the way. He discovered that many illnesses were caused by small organisms, called bacteria. He showed that these bacteria could be made harmless if doctors used antiseptics against them. As a result of Pasteur's discovery, surgeons began to worry much more about hygiene and cleanliness. Pasteur also discovered how to cure the terrible disease of rabies, which people caught when they were bitten by mad dogs. In 1885 he showed how people could be innoculated against the disease. This saved the lives of many people, especially young children, who were often bitten when playing in the streets of large towns.

Another important medical discovery was made by the German scientist Wilhelm Rontgen. He discovered X-rays, and showed how they could be used to photograph the inside of patient's bodies. This made it much easier for doctors to diagnose illnesses.

The Growth of Population

The most important consequence of these discoveries was that people lived longer. Instead of dying from a slight illness they were cured and lived on to a pleasant old age. As a result, the population of Europe grew very quickly. In 1870 there were almost three hundred million people in Europe. By 1914 there were four hundred and twenty million. In all the main countries of Europe there were now more people alive than ever before.

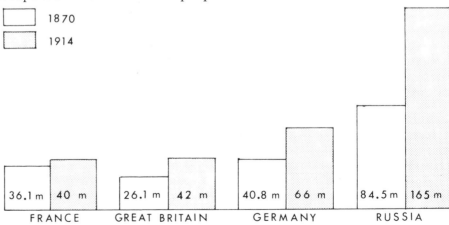

Growth of population in Europe, 1870–1914.

146

The American inventor, Thomas Edison (1847–1931), also invented the forerunner of the modern gramophone record and record player. Here is one of his earliest models—rather different from the modern record player of today! It was on a machine like this that Edison made the first ever record in 1877. What was on the record? Just the five words 'Mary had a little lamb'.

The Discovery of Electricity

New inventions were also made in industry. One of these inventions was electricity. Even the ancient Greeks had heard of electricity, but they had never discovered how to produce it. This was first done by an English scientist, Michael Faraday, in 1831. Some forty years later, in 1871, a Belgian engineer built the first dynamo for producing electricity in large quantities. Soon factory owners began to use electricity instead of steam to drive their machines. It was cheaper, more powerful and more reliable.

People also used electricity for other purposes. In 1879 the American engineer, Thomas Edison, produced the first electric light bulb. Soon the streets of large cities and towns were lit up by electric lights. This made it much more safe and pleasant for people to walk around at night.

A German engineer, Ernst von Siemens, showed how electricity could be used to drive vehicles. In 1879 he invented the first electric tram, which ran along steel rails. By 1900 these trams were in most of the capital cities of

Siemens electric tram in 1879.

147

A later and much larger version—a
Glasgow tram built in 1901.

Europe. They were quieter than horse-drawn cabs, and much faster. They
were also cheap, and many workers travelled on them in order to get to
work. Housewives also travelled into town on them to do their shopping.

The Age of the Motor Car

Another invention, which was even more popular than the tram, was the
motor car. In 1887 a German, Gottlieb von Daimler, produced the first
modern motor car. It had four wheels and was driven by a petrol engine.
Soon other people began to copy his design, and many firms began producing motor cars. Some of these firms are still in business today: Ford, Renault,
Fiat, Daimler, Morris, Austin, Vauxhall, and Rolls-Royce. By 1914 there
were almost a million cars on the roads of Europe.

All these early motor cars were uncomfortable and unreliable machines.
The roads were so bumpy and narrow that they frequently punctured the
tyres. The engines were noisy and often broke down. Many people also
complained that motor cars were dangerous. For a long time in Britain

A German inventor, Karl Benz (1844–1929), specialised in making three-wheeled motor-carriages. This one, made in 1887, cost £140 and could trundle along at 8½ m p h.

Daimler's first four-wheeled motor-car.

An early motor coach tour to Brighton: passengers stop to admire the scenery.

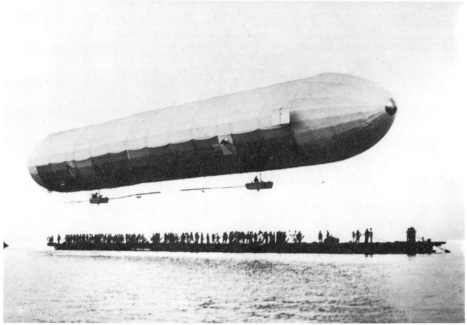

One of Zeppelin's earliest airships pictured in 1900.

Wilbur Wright flying his aeroplane.

motor cars were not allowed to go faster than four miles per hour. Someone even had to walk in front of the car holding a red flag in order to warn people of its approach! However, this law was repealed in 1896 and motor cars were allowed to go as fast as twelve miles per hour. After this they became more popular. People saw that the motor car was a fast and exciting way to travel.

Man takes to the Air

The aeroplane was also invented during these years. Since the eighteenth century people had been able to fly in the air. They did this by using the air balloon. However, air balloons were very slow and they could only go in the direction that the wind was blowing. So in 1900 Count Ferdinand von Zeppelin invented a different machine, called an airship. This floated in the air like a balloon, but also had engines. This enabled it to carry passengers and cargo over long distances.

Meanwhile other people were trying to build aeroplanes. In 1903 two brothers from Ohio in the United States, made the first proper flight in an aeroplane. Their names were Wilbur and Orville Wright. Their flight lasted just fifty-nine seconds! Soon other people made stronger and more powerful aeroplanes, which could fly over longer distances. In 1909 a French pilot, Louis Bleriot, became the first person to fly non-stop across the English

An early photographer was the Englishman W. H. Fox Talbot. Here he is in his back garden organising a picture-taking session; note that the cameras are very similar to Daguerre's (*below*).

Below (right)
Ordinary photographic cameras had existed since the 1820s. Here is an early model, made by the Frenchman Jacques Daguerre.

The typewriter also came into common use towards the end of the nineteenth century. Here is an early model, made of wood in Germany in 1866.

Guglielmo Marconi (1874–1937). Marconi's mother was English but his father was Italian, and he made all of his early experiments with wirelesses in the family home near Bologna in Italy. It was there that he transmitted his first wireless messages in 1896 when he was still only twenty-two years old. However, the Italian government refused to help Marconi to develop his invention, so he went to his relatives in England and set up the world's first wireless signalling company which transmitted messages to and from ships.

Channel. This proved that aeroplanes had a future. By 1914 people had built aeroplanes that could fly over five hundred miles. They were noisy and small. They were often unsafe. But they showed that man could conquer the air.

The Telephone and Wireless

The aeroplane made it possible for people to move around much more quickly than ever before. Two more inventions also helped to speed up communications: the telephone and the wireless. The telephone was first invented by a young American, Alexander Graham Bell, in 1876. It was a wonderful invention. For the first time ever, people could speak to each other even when they were hundreds of miles apart. The first telephones were, of course, very 'crackly'. People had to shout down the mouthpiece in order to be heard. Nevertheless the design of them was soon improved and telephones became very popular.

An Italian engineer, Guglielmo Marconi, made a further step forward. In 1896 he invented a way of sending messages over long distances without using wires. This invention was called 'wireless telegraphy'. In 1901 Marconi sent the first 'wireless messages' across the Atlantic Ocean from Cornwall to Newfoundland. By 1914 a wireless message could be sent all the way round the world in seven minutes. Suddenly the wireless had made the world into a very small and cosy place!

By the end of the nineteenth century great improvements had been made. Here is another typewriter, also German, but made of steel in 1900. Compare it with the one opposite and you will see what great improvements had been made; the 1900 model is very similar to those that we use today. The typewriter did a great deal to improve the status of women, for it created the need for typists and so gave them employment and money.

153

WALKING DRESSES.   FULL DRESS.

LE FOLLET

LE FOLLET

A bird's-eye view of women's fashion and how it changed during the century.

An organ-grinder providing entertainment on the streets of London in the late nineteenth century.

George Bernard Shaw (1856–1950), the Irish playwright and novelist. Shaw wrote many famous works, including *Joan of Arc* and *Pygmalion*, which told of how a learned professor taught a simple flower-girl how to speak 'posh' English. *Pygmalion* has recently been made into a musical called *My Fair Lady*; much of Shaw's original story has been left in, but the ending has been changed from a sad into a happy one.

2   Sport and Entertainment

The inventions that we saw in the last section made life exciting and different. Instead of travelling about on horseback, people could now use motor cars. Instead of sending messages through the post they could use the telephone. If they wanted to go into town to do some shopping, they could take a tram instead of walking.

While all these changes were going on, people also found new things to do in their spare time. The worst years of the Industrial Revolution were over by the end of the nineteenth century. People were beginning to work shorter hours. As they did so, they had more time to relax in the evenings and at weekends. What did they do with this spare time?

A Night at the Theatre

Many people went to the theatre to see a play. In the nineteenth century there were theatres in most towns and the seats were quite cheap. Some people liked to go and see comedies which made them laugh. The best comedies of this time were written by two Irishmen, Oscar Wilde, and George Bernard Shaw. Their plays are still popular today.

Other people went to the theatre to see plays about ghosts and murders. They wanted plays with lots of excitement and violence, so that they could

A tight-rope walker performing his 'death-defying act' in a crowded music hall.

cheer the heroes and boo the villains. Some of the most popular plays were 'The Phantom Breakfast', 'The Death Plank' and 'The Murdering Dentist'. Sometimes the audience was so noisy that the actors could hardly make themselves heard. Nevertheless, everyone enjoyed themselves and went home very contented.

The Old-time Musical Hall

People also liked to go to music halls. There they could watch acrobats, clowns, jugglers, escape artists, singers and comedians. They could laugh at the jokes and join in some of the songs. If they did not like a singer or a comedian they usually booed loudly and threw rotten fruit onto the stage. If they particularly liked someone they threw pennies onto the stage to show their appreciation.

A Night at the 'Movies'

During the 1890s a new form of entertainment was invented which soon rivalled the theatre and the music hall. This was the cinema. The first 'movie' film was made in Paris in 1895. Soon many of them were made and cinemas were built in many towns. All the early films were in black and white and they had no sound. People had to guess what the actors were saying, or read 'subtitles' that were projected onto the screen. Often the film broke down and people had to sit in the dark while it was mended. Nevertheless, this was all part of the fun and the cinema soon became very popular. People queued for hours to see the latest movie!

Theatres, music halls and cinemas kept people happy in the evenings. But what did they do at the weekends?

Potatoes for sale! A scene from a fruit and vegetable market in London in the late nineteenth century. Note all the horse-drawn carts and carriages behind; it took a long time before they were all replaced by motorised lorries and buses.

157

Children lined up at the railway station for a trip to the seaside, all equipped with their buckets and spades!

A Day at the Seaside

Some people went to the seaside. Nowadays we usually spend our holidays at the seaside, lying on the beach and swimming in the sea. Yet it was only in the nineteenth century that people first began to do this. The bathing costumes in those days were quite incredible. People were too shy to show their shoulders, their stomach, or their legs. So they dressed in large bathing costumes that covered most of their body. Women even wore costumes with special corsets so that their waist would look slender. The corsets were made of steel so that they would not get rusty in the water. Sometimes people were even too shy to walk around on the beach in their bathing costume. So they had special bathing huts built which ran on wheels. They changed in them, had them wheeled into the sea, and then took their swim. This way, no one could see them in their bathing costume.

RGATE THE BEACH 2891 X

The Rise of Sport

Swimming in the sea was one way of spending a weekend. Playing sport was another way. Nowadays we are used to watching sport on television or going to watch it at sports grounds. In fact most sports have been played for many hundreds of years. Football and cricket were played in the Middle Ages. Boxing has been going on ever since man first learnt to punch other people. However, it was only in the nineteenth century that most sports were properly organised. Proper sets of rules were drawn up and teams began to play regular matches against each other.

The Early Days of Soccer

Soccer was one of the first sports to be organised in this way. In 1863 the Football Association was established in Britain, to draw up a set of rules for the game. It quickly did this. The rules laid down that each side could have

Margate Beach in the early 1900s. Note the bathing huts wheeled into the sea, and the peculiar prams and push-chairs on the beach. Notice also that although the sun is out nobody is sunbathing; everyone is dressed in their Sunday best with hats and long skirts for the women, and hats, suits, collars and ties for the men. Compare that with the scene on a sunny beach today.

159

A cricket match in England in 1889.

An early boxing match before the Queensberry rules were brought in. Notice how the spectators seem to have joined in and how many of them are women.

no more than eleven players. They also stated what size the pitch had to be and how a goal could be scored. Soon many 'association football' clubs were founded, and in 1872 the first F.A. Cup competition was held. In the same year England and Scotland drew 0-0 in the first ever soccer international. After this people all over Europe began to play soccer. In 1904 the Federation of International Football Associations (F.I.F.A.) was set up. This was a sort of governing body to control soccer all over the world. It still exists today.

Cricket, Tennis and Rugby

Many other sports were as popular as soccer. In cricket the first Test Match was played between England and Australia in Melbourne in 1877. In lawn tennis, the first Wimbledon Championships were held in 1877. Ever since then Wimbledon has been the most important tennis tournament in the world. In rugby, the Rugby Football Association was set up in 1871. It drew up the rules of the game, and established clubs all over the British Isles. Soon rugby came to be played in France, South Africa, Australia and New Zealand.

Boxing

Boxing was another popular sport. In 1867 the Queensberry Rules were drawn up. These laid down how fights should be organised. They stated that boxers should wear padded gloves, and that rounds should only last for three minutes. Soon the heavyweight championships got under way. Most of the good heavyweights before 1914 were from the United States. The best of

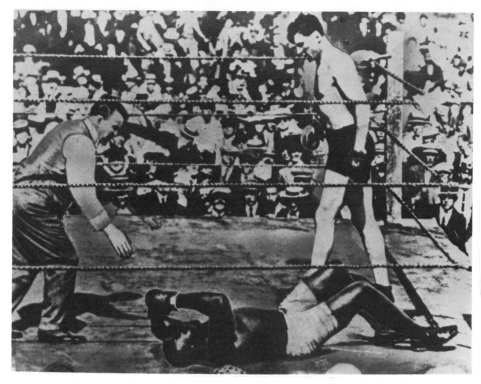

Johnson knocked out by Willard. Notice how Johnson seems to be shielding his eyes from the sun; many people later claimed that he was in fact quite all right and only stayed down on the canvas because he had been bribed to lose the fight. Johnson later denied this and claimed that he had done very little training for the fight and was therefore exhausted by the 26th round.

them was a negro boxer, Jack Johnson, who was heavyweight champion of the world from 1908–15. Johnson was fast and skilful, with a deadly right hand. He finally lost his title in 1915 when he was knocked out by another American, Jess Willard, in the twenty-sixth round of their title fight.

3   The Age of Imperialism

Between 1870 and 1914 Europe became the most powerful continent in the world. Many European countries conquered huge 'empires' in Africa and Asia. They became what we call 'imperial' powers.

Britain had the largest empire. She conquered large parts of Africa and many territories in the Far East. France also built up a large empire for herself. She conquered much of west Africa and also large territories in the Far East (in Indo-China). Germany and Italy also conquered territories in Africa and brought them under their control.

The Reasons for Imperialism

What was the cause of this great rush for overseas empires? In the late nine-

Jack Johnson was one of the greatest heavy-weight boxers of all time. He was widely disliked in the United States because of the fact that he was a Negro, capable of beating the best white men! He died in a car crash in 1946.

One of the most famous administrators of the British Empire, George Nathaniel Curzon (1859–1925). Curzon, who became viceroy of India, is pictured here with his wife and friend in India.

teenth century the factories of Europe were producing more and more goods. This made industrialists and traders look for new regions of the world where they could sell their products and invest their wealth. Africa and Asia seemed to be suitable regions for doing this. Both continents had large numbers of people who could buy European goods. They also had valuable raw materials such as cotton, timber, vegetable oils and minerals. These could be transported to Europe and used in many industries. So, for these reasons, industrialists and traders encouraged their governments to conquer overseas empires.

David Livingstone (1813–73).

Exploring the Unknown

The bravery of many men and women made all these conquests possible. Intrepid explorers travelled where no white man had ever been before. They went up the great rivers of Africa and Asia, hacking their way through the dark and dangerous jungle. They discovered huge lakes and massive, snow-topped mountains. They met the native tribes and made treaties of friendship with the local chiefs. They saw the strange customs of the people and listened to their weird and wonderful languages.

Not all of the explorers survived. Many died from snake-bites or were mauled and killed by lions and tigers. Some lost their way and died in the jungle from starvation or fever. Others were killed by hostile natives. Yet, those who survived and returned to Europe had wonderful stories to tell. They told their fellow-countrymen of the wonder and the riches that they had seen. They encouraged others to become explorers and to find these riches for themselves.

David Livingstone and darkest Africa

One of the bravest explorers was a Scotsman, David Livingstone. Living-

stone came from a poor family and went to work in a cotton mill at the age of ten. He worked hard and soon earned enough money to go to university in Glasgow. At the age of twenty-seven he took a degree in medicine and became a qualified doctor.

Livingstone now had the chance to become a wealthy doctor in his native Scotland. However, he decided instead to become a missionary in Africa. He wanted to convert the Africans to Christianity. In 1840, he made his first voyage to Africa as a member of the London Missionary Society.

Livingstone spent most of the rest of his life in Africa, working as a missionary. He explored vast regions of the country where no white man had ever been. He followed the Zambesi river from its source to the sea. He discovered a huge waterfall in East Africa and called it Victoria Falls after Queen Victoria in England. He became the first white man ever to see the massive Lake Nyasa.

For many years Livingstone sent back news of his discoveries to Britain. However, by 1870, nothing had been heard of him for many years. People began to fear that he was dead—massacred by hostile tribes or killed by a tropical disease. Therefore, in 1870, an American newspaper, the *New York Herald,* sent another explorer, Henry Stanley, to search for Livingstone. After searching for a year, Stanley found a bearded white man at the village of Ujiji, on the shores of Lake Nyasa. He walked up to him and said: 'Doctor Livingstone, I presume?'. Of course he was right. He had found Livingstone alive and well.

Livingstone lived on in Africa for another two years, preaching and healing the sick. He eventually died there in 1873. His death was greatly mourned by the natives who admired his humility and his kindness.

The headquarters of a German colony in East Africa.

Cecil Rhodes and Southern Africa

Another great explorer was Cecil Rhodes. Rhodes was born in the town of Bishop's Stortford in England. He first went to Africa in 1870 to recover from a serious illness. He was only seventeen years old at the time, but quickly made a fortune for himself in diamonds and gold. He owned great mines in the Transvaal and in Rhodesia.

However, Rhodes was not only interested in making money. He also wanted to make Britain the most powerful coloniser in Africa. To do this he wanted to establish a wide belt of British territory, running all the way from Cape (in the south) to Cairo (in the north). There were two small republics which stood in Rhodes' way: the Transvaal and the Orange Free State. These were both inhabited by Dutch settlers, called Boers. The Boers were a proud and hard-working people. They had no intention of giving up their independence.

Cecil Rhodes (1853–1902), British imperialist. When he died Rhodes left a fortune of over £6 million; much of it was given to Oxford University to provide scholarships for students from the Commonwealth, Germany or the U.S.A. to study in England.

An armoured train in South Africa during the Boer War.

The Boer War (1899–1902)

Rhodes therefore decided to go to war against the two Boer republics. The British government gave him their support and sent troops to his aid. In October 1899 war finally broke out. It was known as the 'Boer War'. Both sides fought very savagely and very cruelly. The Boers used 'guerilla' tactics against the British army and killed many soldiers in ambushes. The British retaliated by locking up many Boer families in concentration camps, where twenty thousand people died of hunger and disease.

Eventually, in 1902, the Boers were forced to surrender. By the Peace of Vereeniging (May 1902) they lost their independence. Cecil Rhodes died in the same year. He had realised one of his main ambitions, in bringing the Boers under British control. However, it had been achieved at a terrible price.

A group of Boer guerillas. Note that they have no uniforms—just their guns and a look of determination!

165

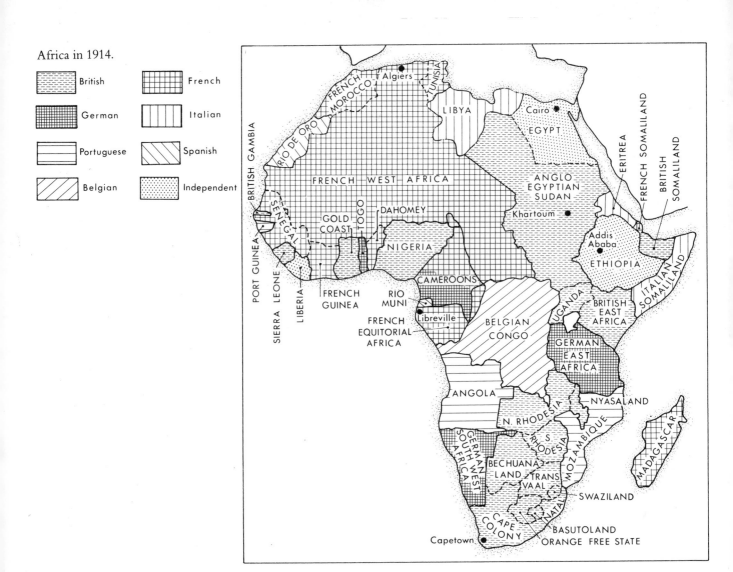

Africa in 1914.

Legend			
British		French	
German		Italian	
Portuguese		Spanish	
Belgian		Independent	

BRITISH GAMBIA
PORT GUINEA
SIERRA LEONE
LIBERIA
SENEGAL
RIO DE ORO
FRENCH MOROCCO
Algiers
TUNISIA
LIBYA
EGYPT
Cairo
ERITREA
FRENCH SOMALILAND
BRITISH SOMALILAND
FRENCH WEST AFRICA
GOLD COAST
TOGO
DAHOMEY
NIGERIA
FRENCH GUINEA
ANGLO EGYPTIAN SUDAN
Khartoum
Addis Ababa
ETHIOPIA
ITALIAN SOMALILAND
CAMEROONS
RIO MUNI
Libreville
FRENCH EQUITORIAL AFRICA
BELGIAN CONGO
UGANDA
BRITISH EAST AFRICA
GERMAN EAST AFRICA
ANGOLA
N. RHODESIA
NYASALAND
GERMAN SOUTH WEST AFRICA
S. RHODESIA
BECHUANA-LAND
TRANS VAAL
MOZAMBIQUE
SWAZILAND
NATAL
CAPE COLONY
BASUTOLAND
ORANGE FREE STATE
MADAGASCAR
Capetown

By 1914 over nine-tenths of Africa was ruled by major European powers. Most of Asia was also under European control. Never before in the history of man had Europe been so powerful as she was in this 'age of imperialism'.

Some Remarks on Imperialism

There is one thing that we should notice about all these conquests. The people of Asia and Africa did not want to be ruled by Europeans. They did not want to lose their freedom, but they were too weak to resist. Their spears and swords were no match for the ships, cannon and guns of the European in-

vaders. It is not surprising therefore that the Asians and Africans soon hated the Europeans, and plotted to drive them out of their homeland. Most of the empires that were won between 1870 and 1914 no longer exist today. The age of imperialism therefore only lasted for a short time.

During the late nineteenth century primary education was made compulsory in most European countries. However, the schools were often not very good and the classes were very large. How about this for a drawing lesson?

TO DO

1 Find out more about the life and work of Louis Pasteur. Use an encyclopedia to help you do this.
2 Many of the early motor car manufacturers are still in business today. Try to find out something about their history and the cars that they have produced over the years. If necessary, write to the manufacturers that you are studying and ask for information.
3 Write a short history of your favourite sport. When did it start? When were proper rules for it established? Who were its most famous stars?
4 Find out if your local religious order has missionaries in Africa or Asia. If it has, try to discover when it first sent missionaries there and what sort of work they did.
5 Write the story of the life of David Livingstone.
6 Take a map of modern Africa and compare it with the map of Africa in 1914 which is on page 166. In what way has Africa changed since 1914? Make a list of the new states that have been established there, and note down to which countries they used to belong.

TO READ

The Motor Revolution, Then and There Series, David St. J. Thomas, Longman Group.

From Kitty Hawk to Outer Space. The Story of the Aeroplane, L. E. Snellgrove, Longman Group, 2nd edition.

From Steamcarts to Minicars. A History of Motor Cars, L. E. Snellgrove, Longman Group.

Modern Africa 1870–1970, Barry Williams, Longman Group.

The British in Egypt, W. K. Ritchie, Longman Group.

The Motor Industry, Jackdaw Series no. 77, Jackdaw Publications.

Pasteur and the Germ Theory, Jackdaw Series no. 84, Jackdaw Publication .

Faraday and Electricity, Jackdaw Series no. 86, Jackdaw Publications.

Cricket, Jackdaw Series no. 101, Jackdaw Publications.

Soccer, Jackdaw Series no. 104, Jackdaw Publications.

The Voyages of Captain Cook, Jackdaw Series no. 20, Jackdaw Publications.

The Anglo-Boer War, Jackdaw Series no. 68, Jackdaw Publications.

DATELINE

1831	Faraday produces electricity.
1840	Livingstone first goes to Africa.
1863	Founding of the Football Association.
1867	Queensberry rules drawn up for boxing.
1871	Founding of the Rugby Football Association.
	Invention of the dynamo.
1872	The first F.A. Cup Final.
1876	Alexander Bell invents the telephone.
1877	The first cricket Test Match between England and Australia.
	The first Wimbledon Lawn Tennis Championships.
1879	Thomas Edison invents the electric light bulb.
1885	Louis Pasteur discovers a cure for rabies.
1887	Daimler builds the first modern motor car.
1895	The first movie pictures are shown in Paris.
1896	Marconi invents the wireless.
1899	The outbreak of the Boer War.
1900	The first Zeppelin airship.
1901	The first wireless message crosses the Atlantic.
1902	The Peace of Vereeniging brings an end to the Boer War.
1903	The Wright brothers make the first aeroplane flight.
1909	Louis Bleriot makes the first flight across the English Channel.

8   The First World War, 1914–18

For almost the whole of the nineteenth century there was no major war in Europe. There was peace for almost one hundred years. Then in 1914 war finally broke out. Soon all the major European powers were involved. This was the First World War and it lasted for over four years. Millions of people were killed in it and thousands of villages and houses were destroyed. It was the most terrible war that Europe had ever seen.

In this chapter you will read about the First World War. You will see what caused it, how it was fought and how peace was finally restored.

'The most terrible war that Europe had ever seen'.

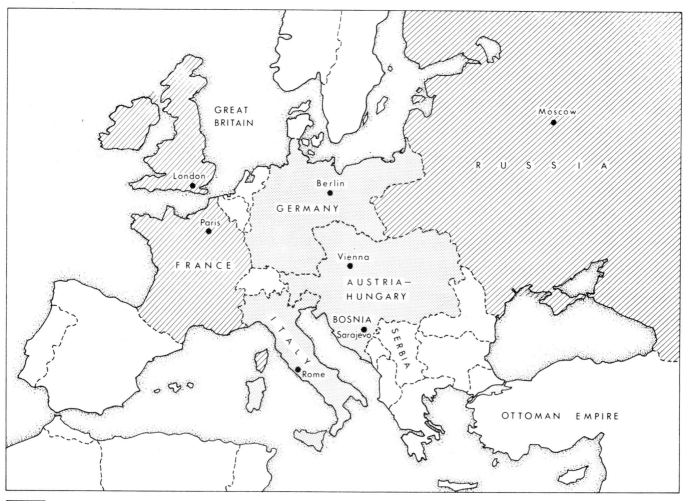

1 *Murder at Sarajevo*

Earlier in this book you read how Otto von Bismarck united Germany. You learnt how he finally brought this about by defeating France in the Franco-Prussian War of 1870–71. Now you will see how this defeat of France was one of the causes of a much more terrible war that broke out in 1914.

The Triple Alliance

The French people never forgave Germany for defeating them in the Franco-Prussian War. Neither did they forgive Germany for taking over two of

France's eastern provinces, Alsace and Lorraine. They were determined that one day France would gain her revenge. Because of this, Germany decided to make sure that she had allies, to defend her against a possible French attack. So in 1882 she formed an alliance with Austria and Italy. This was called the Triple Alliance. Each of the three countries promised to come to the aid of the others if they were attacked by a foreign power.

The 'Entente Cordiale'

France was alarmed by this alliance. She feared that it made Germany more powerful than ever before. Therefore she decided to protect herself by forming her own alliance with Russia. In 1904, she made a treaty of friendship with Britain, which was called the *Entente Cordiale* (the friendly agreement). The agreements between France, Russia and Britain were soon known as the Triple *Entente* (the triple agreement).

The Triple Alliance and the Triple *Entente* were only defensive alliances. They only came into effect if one country was actually attacked by a foreign power. Nevertheless, if a country from one alliance attacked a country from the other alliance, then all six countries would probably end up at war. This was an extremely dangerous situation.

Alfred Krupp (1812–87) had taken over his father's small steelworks at Essen when only fourteen years old. He developed it into a great works which played an important part in the arming of Germany.

By the beginning of the twentieth century the German shipbuilding industry was highly efficient. Here is the steamship *Kaiser Wilhelm II*, the largest steamship in the world when she was launched in 1902.

171

Interior of the Krupps steelworks where many of the large guns used in the First World War were made.

The Arms Race

The situation was made worse by the 'arms race', as all six countries began to strengthen their armed forces. The arms race really began in the 1890s, between Britain and Germany. At this time the British navy was the largest and most powerful navy in the world. Britain needed it for her defence because she was an island. She also needed it to protect her trade with her overseas empire.

However, in 1897 the German Parliament passed a Naval Law. This increased the size and strength of the German navy. Germany wanted to show the world that she could be a great power at sea as well as on land. Britain, quite naturally, saw this as a threat to her own naval superiority. Therefore in 1905 the British government decided to build two new battleships. They

The first of the 'dreadnoughts'—HMS Dreadnought, launched in 1907.

were called the Dreadnoughts. They were larger and more powerful than any other ship afloat.

Germany was determined not to be outdone. So, in 1907, she also began to build Dreadnoughts. Soon both countries were racing to build ships faster than the other. France, Austria, Russia and Italy did the same. The arms race was on, and governments spent increasing amounts of money on their armed forces. They were determined to be well prepared in case war broke out.

The arms race caused a great deal of excitement at the time, as people urged their governments to spend more and more money on arms. It also encouraged a sense of rivalry between the two sets of alliances. Everyone began to get the feeling that war could not be far away.

Alfred von Tirpitz (1849–1930), father of the German navy.

The Problem of Serbia

The event which finally caused the outbreak of war took place in the Balkans. If you look at the map on page 174 you will see that there were many small states in the Balkan peninsula. The most powerful of these states was Serbia. Serbia was the home of the Serbian nationalists. They wanted to bring all Serbs, throughout the Balkan peninsula, under Serbian rule. Many Serbs lived in the small state of Bosnia, which was ruled by Austria. Serbia therefore wanted to annex or take over Bosnia. She was supported by Russia. Russia wanted to extend her influence in the Balkans and to weaken the influence of Austria. She knew that if Serbia succeeded in annexing Bosnia, then Austria's influence in the Balkans would be finished.

The Balkan States in 1914.

Austria had no intention of allowing Serbia to take over Bosnia. She was prepared to go to war to prevent it. In 1914 she found the chance to do this.

Murder at Sarajevo

On 28 June 1914 the Archduke Franz Ferdinand, heir to the throne of Austria, paid a visit to Bosnia. He rode through the streets of Sarajevo, the capital of Bosnia, in an open car. His wife was beside him, and cheering crowds lined the streets. Then two shots rang out. The archduke and his wife slumped forward in their seats. The archduke had been shot in the head and his wife had been shot in the neck. Within half-an-hour they were both dead.

The man who had fired the shots was a Serbian nationalist, Gavrilo Princip. He was a member of a Serbian terrorist organisation called the

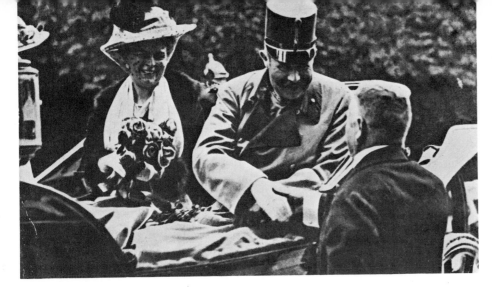

A picture of the Archduke Franz Ferdinand and his wife taken as they began their fatal drive through the streets of Sarajevo.

'Black Hand'. The Austrian government therefore blamed Serbia for the assassination of the archduke. It decided that the time had come to defeat Serbia once and for all. Germany promised Austria her full support if she went to war. So on 28 July 1914 Austria declared war on Serbia.

The Outbreak of War

When Austria declared war, Russia immediately mobilised her forces in defence of Serbia. This brought Austria into direct conflict with Russia. Austria was supported by her ally in the Triple Alliance, Germany. Russia was supported by her allies in the Triple *Entente*, France and Britain. By 4 August 1914 all the major countries of Europe were at war. The First World War had begun.

The arrest of Gavrilo Princip.

2 The War becomes a Stalemate

When war broke out in 1914 thousands of men in all countries volunteered to join the army. They were certain that their country was fighting for a good cause. They also thought that the war would be all over within a few months. Even the politicians and the generals thought in terms of a short war and rapid victory. Soon they were to realise how wrong they were.

The Failure of the Schlieffen Plan

The Schlieffen Plan.

Most of the early fighting in the war took place in France. The German army

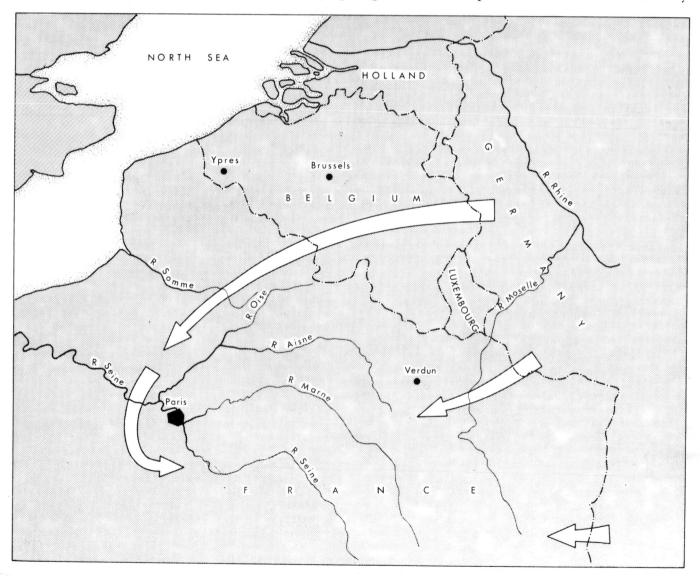

DESIGNED BY LT GEN SIR R.S.S BADEN POWELL

Are YOU in this?

As soon as war broke out, all countries began recruiting soldiers as quickly as they could. Here are two typical recruiting posters calling on people to serve their country. At first many thousands of people came forward, but, as the war dragged on and the deaths mounted, many became sick of war and the destruction that it brought.

"YOUR COUNTRY NEEDS YOU"

177

commanders pinned all their hopes on a swift victory over the French. They hoped to get this victory by using a special plan called the Schlieffen Plan. By this the German armies would march through Belgium into northern France and capture Paris. France would then be forced to surrender.

At first everything went according to plan. The German armies swept into France and forced the French armies to retreat towards Paris. British forces, which had been rushed across the Channel to France, were unable to slow down the German advances. Then, when the German armies were in sight of Paris, the French made one last effort. At the Battle of the Marne (6–13

The Western Front, 1914–15.

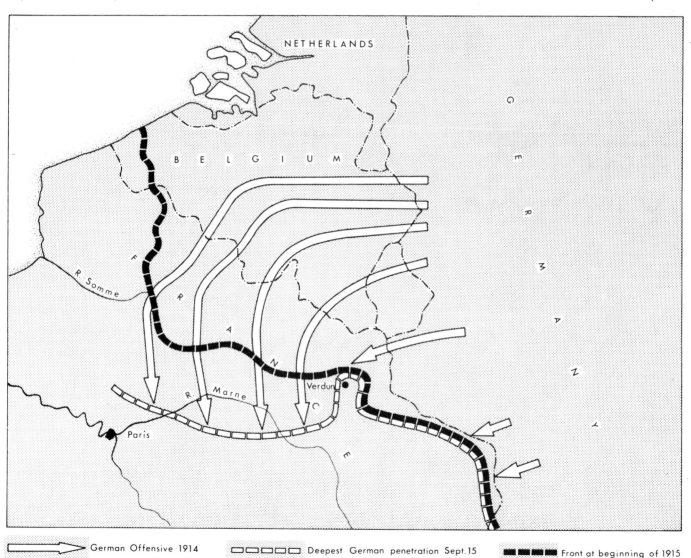

German Offensive 1914   Deepest German penetration Sept. 15   Front at beginning of 1915

A German artillery position.

September) they defeated the Germans in a week of fierce fighting. The German armies retreated a few miles and dug themselves into trenches. The French and British armies did the same. Soon both sides faced each other across the 'no-man's land' that separated the two lines of trenches.

Life in the Trenches

Trench warfare was to last on the western front for the next three years. The trenches were deep enough for men to move around in them without being seen by the enemy. They were defended by strongly-built machine gun posts that looked out over 'no-man's land'. Whenever enemy troops wanted to attack they first had to cross no-man's land. They were always met with a hail of machine gun bullets. Thousands were killed and wounded. Few ever got through to the enemy trenches. This meant that neither side was able to advance very far. The war quickly became a deadlock.

German troops use a flame thrower, trying to force the enemy to leave their trenches.

'Soon both sides faced each other across the "no-man's land" that separated the two lines of trenches' —French trenches in 1915.

Opposite (bottom)
Ringing the bell to warn of a gas attack. Note the gas mask pulled tightly over the soldier's head.

A short rest and a bite to eat before the next attack, and possible death. British soldiers in their trenches in 1915.

180

Deadly new Weapons

The generals on both sides tried hard to find a way of breaking this deadlock. In April 1915 the Germans started to use poison gas. This choked and blinded many British and French troops. Soon they were supplied with gas masks, and these gave them some protection. Sometimes the wind changed direction so that the gas was blown back into the faces of the German troops. They then had to put on their own gas masks before it was too late.

Both sides also used airships and aeroplanes for bombing raids. Three Zeppelins even bombed some towns in England. The airships were very slow and the aeroplanes rather flimsy. Consequently neither did very much harm.

The tank was a much more dangerous weapon. The British invented this, and used it for the first time in 1916. It had powerful guns and was well protected against enemy bullets. However, it was a long time before soldiers learnt how to use it properly.

The Battle of Verdun

Two of the most terrible battles of the whole war took place in 1916. In the first, the Battle of Verdun, the Germans tried to capture the important French fortress of Verdun. In January they began to bombard the fortress with their heavy artillery. However, the French were determined that Verdun should not surrender. Their leader, General Pétain, proudly said: 'They shall not

A machine gun post ready for action.

181

Even horses had to be provided with gas masks. German troops moving to the front.

Opposite (top)
The tangled mass of barbed wire in 'no-man's land' between the two lines of trenches.

Opposite (bottom)
A machine gun post ready for a gas attack.

'Sometimes the gas was blown back into the face of the troops'. British dispatch riders beat a hasty retreat.

pass!' The troops fought bravely and refused to give in. In July the Germans were forced to call off their attack. The French still held Verdun, but over three hundred and fifty thousand men had died in its defence.

The Battle of the Somme

The second battle in 1916 was the Battle of the Somme. In this the British and French armies tried to break through the German defences in the valley of the river Somme. The battle started on 1 July as huge guns bombarded the German trenches. Then thousands of troops charged across no-man's land to press home the attack. The German troops defended bravely and fought every inch of the way. The battle raged from July until late October. When

A British aeroplane of the First World War—only for the brave!

Opposite (top)
A Zeppelin in 1917, equipped for bombing missions.

Opposite (bottom)
A large field gun of the German heavy artillery.

Sometimes the old horse could last longer than the modern invention! A field ambulance plods slowly past a bombed-out tank.

A large British field gun being slowly dragged through the thick clogging mud towards the front.

it ended the British and French had advanced about four miles. But they had lost six hundred thousand men, dead or wounded. The Germans lost the same number. For both sides it was a terrible price to pay for four miles of muddy ground.

The Russian 'Steamroller' breaks down

In eastern Europe, Russia fought against the combined armies of Germany and Austria. Russia's armies were huge. People often called them the 'Russian Steamroller'. They hoped that the 'steamroller' would roll forward into

One of the largest French guns, a 340 millimetre field gun, mounted on tracks so that it could be easily moved about.

French troops on the retreat in April 1916.

Europe and crush the German and Austrian resistance. However, this did not happen. The Russian troops were badly trained and they had very old-fashioned equipment. Soon they suffered many terrible defeats and were forced to retreat into Russia. Thousands of men were killed in battle, shot down by the accurate fire of the German guns. Nevertheless, Russia refused to surrender. Her armies were hard pressed, but did not give up the fight. Germany and Austria could not achieve the breakthrough that they wanted.

Fixing their bayonets into place, troops get ready to go over the top into 'no man's land'.

HMS *Erin*, a ship of the British Royal Navy built in 1915.

The Battle of Jutland, 31 May 1916.

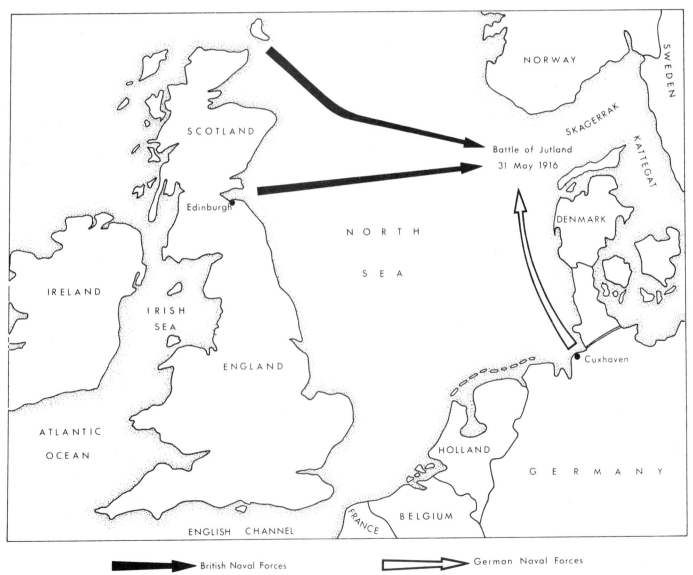

Not all U-boats were successful. Here one surrenders to the British trawler, the *Lady Shirley*, and her crew is taken prisoner.

The War at Sea

Many people thought that the decisive battles of the war would be fought at sea. You will remember that Britain and Germany had spent millions of pounds on their navies before the war. They had both built huge Dreadnoughts. Now they hoped to show that this expenditure had been worthwhile.

As soon as war started the British navy blockaded the German ports. It did this to stop all supplies of food and equipment getting through, and hoped that when Germany ran short of these she would be forced to surrender. The Germans retaliated by using their U-boats (submarines) against British and French cargo ships. The U-boats operated in the Atlantic off the west coast of Ireland. They sank many ships, ruining their cargo and killing their crew.

The Sinking of the 'Lusitania'

In May 1915 a German U-boat torpedoed the passenger liner the *Lusitania* bound for Liverpool from New York. The torpedo smashed a huge hole in the ship's side and it sank immediately. The passengers had no chance to escape and over one thousand of them were drowned. The news of the sinking of the *Lusitania* caused a great outcry in the United States, because many of those drowned were American. Germany did not wish to give the United States any reason for joining the war against her. So she called off the U-boat campaign. This meant that French and British ships could once again sail the Atlantic in safety.

The Battle of Jutland

Meanwhile the main German fleet did nothing during the first two years of the war. The huge Dreadnoughts stayed at anchor in the ports of Germany. They could not put to sea without risking a battle with the British fleet. This was anchored in the Scottish ports of Scapa Flow and Rosyth, waiting for the German ships to appear.

A German propaganda poster: 'God punish England'. All countries believed that they were in the right and that God was on their side.

The French Prime Minister, Georges Clemenceau, visiting French troop positions in 1917. At the time this picture was taken Clemenceau was seventy-six years old, but he had the nickname 'The Tiger' and did much to keep alive the French spirit of resistance during the war.

Everyone deserves a rest now and again! German troops take shelter in a shell hole while their companions keep watch.

In May 1916, the German vice-admiral Scheer grew tired of this deadlock and decided to try to break free. He therefore gave the order for his ships to move out to sea. The British quickly spotted this and moved forward to stop them. The two fleets met in the Battle of Jutland on the evening of 31 May. It was a fierce and hectic battle. When darkness eventually came, the British fleet had suffered the greater casualties. It had lost fourteen ships, while the German fleet had lost only eleven. Nevertheless, vice-admiral Scheer saw that he could not win a decisive victory. So the German fleet returned to port and stayed there for the rest of the war. Because of this the Battle of Jutland is usually regarded as a British victory.

Because so many men were away at the front, women were needed to take over their jobs in factories, producing war equipment. Here are some at work in a gas-mask factory; note the stern looks of the two supervisors.

Women working in a munitions factory.

Women driving an ambulance near the war front. Because they did so many vital jobs during the war, women came to be considered as having a vital role to play in society. So, when the war ended, women were given the vote in many European countries and began to be treated as the equals of men.

Deadlock in 1916

As 1916 drew to a close the war seemed completely deadlocked. The troops on the western front sat huddled together in their flooded trenches. The Russians on the eastern front shivered in the winter snow and frost. The sailors in the British and German navies looked out to sea, waiting for something to happen. All of them hoped that the war would end soon. Yet no one had any idea which side would win.

3 Victory and Peace

In January 1917 the German government took an important decision which changed the whole course of the war. They decided to order their U-boats to sink all ships that did trade with Britain and France. By doing this they hoped to starve the two countries of food and equipment. Then they would be forced to surrender. The German government pinned all their hopes on this policy. It was their 'short-cut' to victory.

The United States joins the War

The U-boats did their job well. Between January and April 1917 they torpedoed over six hundred merchant ships in the Atlantic. They all sank, carrying their cargo and their sailors to the bottom of the ocean. Soon Britain began to run short of food stocks and the government became very worried. The German short-cut seemed to be working.

However, the Germans made one simple mistake. They torpedoed many American ships that were trading with Britain and France. This annoyed many people in the United States. They began to demand that the United States declare war on Germany and gain revenge for the sinking of their ships.

President Woodrow Wilson had always wanted the United States to keep out of the war. He thought that the countries of Europe should be left to settle their own quarrels without help from outside. However, the U-boat attacks on American ships made him change his mind. On 2 April 1917 he asked Congress to declare war on Germany. These were his words:

> Vessels of every kind, whatever their flag, their character, their cargo, their destination, their errand, have been ruthlessly sent to the bottom without warning and without thought of help or mercy for those on board, the vessels of friendly neutrals along with those of belligerents . . . The world must be made safe for democracy . . .

Shouts of joy and approval greeted the President's words, and Congress declared war on Germany. Soon great quantities of American arms and equipment were shipped to Europe.

'By the spring of 1918 thousands of American troops were beginning to arrive in France'.

German troops on the eastern front in Poland. Fighting stopped here after the Treaty of Brest-Litovsk in March 1918.

The Collapse of Russia

The entry of the United States into the war could not have come at a better time. In October 1917 there was a communist revolution in Russia which overthrew the government of the Tsar. Six months later the new rulers of Russia signed a truce with Germany, the Treaty of Brest–Litovsk (March 1918). By this Russia withdrew from the war. (See chapter 9, section 2).

Germany now had the chance to move thousands of troops to the western front. If she had been able to do this a year earlier she would have been able to defeat Britain and France. However, it was already too late. By the spring of 1918 thousands of American troops were beginning to arrive in France. They brought with them fresh equipment and supplies. This strengthened the British and French armies and gave their weary troops fresh hope.

The Final Battles

Between March and August 1918 the German armies tried desperately to achieve a breakthrough. They threw all their men and equipment into one last effort to reach Paris and force France to surrender. However, they failed. On 8 August the British, French and American troops launched a strong counter-attack. This forced the Germans to leave their trenches and to retreat towards Belgium. The German commanders then realised that they could not avoid defeat. So, on 11 November 1918, Germany surrendered. The armistice was signed at eleven in the morning. It was the eleventh hour of the eleventh day of the eleventh month of the year. Germany's ally, Austria, had already surrendered the year before. Europe was now at peace.

The Peace Conference at Paris

When the war was over a special conference was held in Paris to draw up the terms of peace. The leaders of all the victorious nations were there.

President Wilson came all the way from the United States to attend the conference. When he arrived in Paris, people lined the streets to cheer him. They were grateful to the United States for joining them in the war against Germany. President Wilson had already drawn up a peace programme that he called his Fourteen Points. Now he tried to persuade the leaders of other countries to accept this programme as a basis for peace.

Georges Clemenceau negotiated for France. He had been Prime Minister of the country during the last years of the war. He was known as the 'Tiger'. He was determined that Germany should be made pay for the damage that her armies had caused in France. He also wanted to make sure that Germany would never again be strong enough to cause a war in Europe.

David Lloyd George was Britain's representative at the peace conference.

He had been Prime Minister since 1916. He was a clever politician and people often called him the 'Welsh wizard'. Britain had gone heavily into debt in order to pay for her war effort. She had also lost much of her trade with the rest of the world. Lloyd George therefore agreed with Clemenceau. He wanted to make sure that Germany paid compensation for the damage that she had done. Some newspapers in Britain said that he should 'squeeze Germany until the pips squeak'!

The negotiations at Versailles started in January 1919. They went on for over a year. Many separate treaties were drawn up. Each of them dealt with a separate country.

The Treaty of Versailles

The treaty that dealt with Germany was called the Treaty of Versailles. By this Germany lost some of her territory to France, Belgium and Poland. Her army was reduced in size to one hundred thousand men, and she was not allowed to have troops within fifty kilometres of her frontier with France. This strip of fifty kilometres was called the 'demilitarised zone'. Finally the treaty held Germany was responsible for causing the war. She was therefore ordered to pay compensation for all the damage that she had caused. A special commission was set up to decide the amount that she would pay.

Lost by Germany	Lost by Russia	Lost by Austria–Hungary	Rhineland Zone of Allied occupation
Lost by Bulgaria	Plebiscite areas ceded or retained by the League of Nations		

The Treaty of Saint-Germain

The treaty that dealt with the Austrian Empire was called the Treaty of Saint-Germain. It divided the Empire into several independent countries. This was largely President Wilson's idea. He wanted all the nationalities in the Austrian

The official signing of the Treaty of Versailles on 28 June 1919. It took place in the Hall of Mirrors at Versailles where, in January 1871 after the Franco-Prussian war, King William I of Prussia had been crowned as German Emperor. In this way France's revenge for her defeat in 1871 was complete for the German Empire was now defeated.

Empire to have self-government. Austria herself was left in existence but she was made very much smaller. Hungary was also greatly reduced in size. The rest of the Empire was then divided between three new countries: Yugoslavia (in the south), Czechoslovakia and Poland (in the north).

The League of Nations

The negotiators at Versailles also set up an organisation called the League of Nations. This was also President Wilson's idea. It was a kind of international parliament where states could meet together and settle their disputes with one another. Everyone hoped that the League would encourage states to negotiate with one another rather than go to war. They hoped that it would preserve peace in Europe. The League's headquarters were at Geneva. It started its meetings in 1920.

First session of the League of Nations at San Sebastian in August 1920.

When the negotiators finally left Paris they were satisfied with the work that they had done. They had punished Germany. They had solved the problem of the old Austrian Empire. They had set up the League of Nations to prevent war breaking out in the future. In later years people were to accuse them of making many mistakes. But for the moment all seemed well.

The Problems of Peace

The war was over. Peace had come at last. People now faced the task of re-building Europe. Over ten million people had died during the fighting. Most of them had been young men whose skill and energy would now be badly missed. Hundreds of houses and villages had been destroyed by bombs and shells. They now had to be rebuilt. Most countries had gone heavily into debt in order to pay for their war effort. Those debts had now to be repaid. It was obviously going to be a long time before life in Europe would get back to normal.

TO DO

1 You are a newspaper reporter and you saw the assassination at Sarajevo. Write a report of the event for your readers. Tell them what results you think that it will have in Europe.
2 Draw up a list of the major events and battles of the war. Which battles, in your opinion, were the most important?
3 You are one of the soldiers in the trenches on the western front. Write some letters home telling your wife what life is like in the trenches.
4 Make a list of the tactics and weapons that Napoleon used in his battles (see chapter 3). Then make a list of those used in the First World War. What were the main differences?

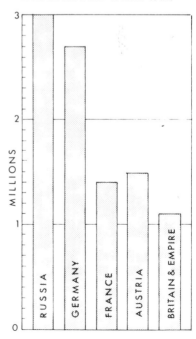

Deaths in the First World War.

Rupert Brooke (1887–1915), an English poet who was killed in action during the First World War. One of his most famous poems, *The Soldier*, written in 1914, begins with these words:

If I should die, think only this of me:
That there's some corner of a foreign
* field*
That is for ever England. There shall be
In that rich earth a dust concealed;
A dust whom England bore, shaped,
* made aware,*
Gave, once, her flowers to love, her
* ways to roam,*
A body of England's, breathing English
* air,*
Washed by the rivers, blest by suns of
* home.*

Brooke supported the war, and thought that it would bring out the best in man. Other poets, however, soon thought differently and wrote about the evils and horrors of so much death and destruction.

5   Try to find out more about the aeroplanes that were used in the First World War. How fast could they go? How far could they fly?

TO READ

World War One, Modern Times, S. R. Gibbons and P. Morican, Longman Group.
Bismarck, the Kaiser and Germany, B. J. Elliott, Longman Group.
The First World War, Richard Musman, Chatto and Windus Educational.
Europe, Making the Modern World, John Robottom (ed.), Longman Group.
Memoirs of an Infantry Officer, Seigfried Sassoon.
Assassination at Sarajevo, Jackdaw Series no. 37, Jackdaw Publications.
The Somme, Jackdaw Series no 111, Jackdaw Publications.

DATELINE

1882	The Triple Alliance (Austria, Italy and Germany).
1904	The *Entente Cordiale* (Britain and France).
1907	The Triple *Entente* (Britain, France and Russia).
1914	28 June: Archduke Franz Ferdinand assassinated at Sarajevo.
	4 August: the First World War begins.
	6–13 September: the battle of the Marne.
1915	The sinking of the *Lusitania*.
1916	January–July: the Battle of Verdun.
	May: the Battle of Jutland.
	July–October: the Battle of the Somme.
1917	The United States of America joins the war.
1918	March: Russia and Germany sign the Treaty of Brest Litovsk.
	November: Germany surrenders—the war is over.
1919	The peace negotiations in Paris.

9   The Inter-War Years, 1919–39

The years between 1919 and 1939 are often called the 'inter-war years'. This is because they come between the end of the First World War and the beginning of the Second World War. For most people they were not happy years. An economic crisis, called the Great Depression, made many industries bankrupt and threw millions of people out of work. Meanwhile in many countries dictators came to power, who did away with democratic government.

In this chapter we shall look at the problems of the Great Depression. We shall also examine the rise of dictatorships in Russia, Italy and Germany.

The Great Depression threw millions of people out of work. Here unemployed workers queue up for food.

Jobs were hard to find after the war: a queue outside a poor relief soup kitchen in 1924.

1 Europe and the Great Depression

After the war it took a long time for life to return to normal. Factories had to be started up again. Shops and houses had to be rebuilt. Men had to leave the army and find themselves jobs in civilian life. This was not always easy. The war had caused great destruction and jobs were hard to find.

Post-war Recovery

Nevertheless, during the 1920s things did begin to improve. Factories began production again and the shops were soon full of customers. Men began to find employment and forgot about the troubles of war. Much of this im-

A night café on wheels, offering free soup to those in need. Note that most of these people are not tramps or down-and-outs, but just ordinary people who had no chance of finding a job.

provement was caused by money that came from the United States. You will remember that the United States only entered the war in 1917. It did not have to spend as much money on the war effort as countries in Europe did. Neither did it suffer from any battles or bombing. Therefore, the United States remained prosperous while the countries of Europe were poor. Americans had plenty of money to spare. Once the war was over they invested much of this money in Europe. Many of the industries that started up in Europe were financed by money from the United States.

The Wall Street Crash

Then in 1929 there was a catastrophe. There was a terrible crisis in the United States. Americans began to lose confidence in some of their leading companies. They feared that these companies would go bankrupt. Therefore, they began to sell their stocks and shares. Soon many companies went out of business. They were forced to close down because no one would invest money in them. As a result many millions of workers lost their jobs. This crisis was known as the 'Wall Street Crash' because the stocks and shares market was on Wall Street in New York.

The Great Depression

When the crisis started in the United States, Americans also began to withdraw the money that they had invested in Europe. Many European industries had to pay back their loans. As a result they also went bankrupt and had to close down. Millions of workers lost their jobs. By 1933 there were almost

The Jarrow marchers arrive in London in the pouring rain in 1936.

thirty million workers unemployed in Europe and the United States. This became known as the Great Depression.

The Great Depression lasted for most of the 1930s. Most people were bored and frustrated as well as being short of money. They wanted to work but there were no jobs to be had. All they could do was to sit around on street corners, talking to friends and complaining about the hard times. They could not even afford to go to the local pub for a drink because they did not have enough money. Most people had to make do with second-hand clothes.

Imagine what life was like in the town of Jarrow in north-east England! In 1933 the local shipyard had to close down because it ran out of orders. This left eighty per cent of the men in the town without jobs. The streets were full of people walking around with nothing to do. In 1936 two hundred men from the town marched nearly three hundred miles to London, to present a petition to the Prime Minister. They wanted the government to provide them with jobs, but the government could do nothing to help.

People have long memories. Many people alive today remember what the Great Depression was like. They remember it as a time of poverty and of boredom. Nevertheless, despite these problems, there was a brighter side to life.

Rudolf Valentino, Italian film star of the silent movies in the 1920s.

Motor Cars

For one thing, motor cars were becoming more common. This was largely due to an American car manufacturer, Henry Ford. In his factory in Detroit, he showed that motor cars could be made cheaply and efficiently by means of 'mass production'. Soon car manufacturers in Europe followed his example. They made small cars which were cheap to buy and economical to run. This meant that more people than ever before could afford to buy a car. By 1939

Mass production at the Austin factory in England in the 1930s.

there were over five million cars on the roads of Europe—five times more than there had been in 1914.

The Radio

The radio was also very popular. We saw earlier that Marconi sent the first wireless message in 1901. (see chapter 7). After the First World War radio stations were set up in many countries to broadcast programmes. The B.B.C. (British Broadcasting Corporation) was founded in 1922. Radio Telefís Éireann started its broadcasts a few years later. Soon millions of people throughout Europe had a radio set. In the evenings they could sit at home in comfort and listen to a good play or some music. In this way the radio brought entertainment and amusement to many people in their own homes.

The Television

A Scotsman, John Logie Baird, went a stage further than the radio. In 1914 he invented the television. The first television sets were very unreliable. The picture was very bad and they often broke down. However, they were soon improved. In 1936 the B.B.C. opened up the first television service in Europe. At this stage only very rich people could afford to buy a set, as they were very expensive. Yet, everyone could see that television had a great future ahead of it.

Mary Pickford, glamour girl of the early cinema.

'Talkies' at the Cinema

During the 1930s many people liked to go out in the evenings to the cinema. We saw earlier that the first movie films were made before the First World War. All these early films had no sound, they just had subtitles which told the audience what the actors were saying. Then, in 1927, the first film with

Mickey Mouse. © *Walt Disney Productions*.

Charlie Chaplin, the English film comedian, who made millions of people laugh at the adventures and misfortunes of poor 'Charlie' in the silent films of the 1920s.

James Cagney *(left)*

Humphrey Bogart *(right)*

Bing Crosby, American singer and film star. Famous for his 'crooning' voice, Crosby's recording of the song *White Christmas* is the biggest selling record ever made.

sound was made. It was a great success although the sound was very 'crackly'. From then on all films were 'talkies' and the cinema became more popular than ever before.

The best talkie films were all made at Hollywood in the United States. Bing Crosby was one of the most famous singing stars. People also loved Fred Astaire who danced in many 'musicals'. Films about 'gangsters' were also very popular. The most exciting ones were made by Humphrey Bogart and James Cagney. They always played the part of ruthless villains, but they never got away with their crimes! People also liked the cartoon films of Mickey Mouse and Donald Duck, made by Walt Disney. In 1937 Disney also made the film 'Snow White and the Seven Dwarfs', which is still very popular today.

'Jazz' Music

Music was another form of entertainment. Nowadays we listen to 'pop' music. In the 1920s our fathers and grandfathers listened to 'jazz' and 'swing'. It was happy music with lots of rhythm and noise so that people could dance to it. The most famous jazz musicians were Louis Armstrong, 'Jelly-Roll'

The clarinettist Benny Goodman with his band in the 1930s. Goodman's music was different from that of Armstrong: sweet and pleasant on the ear, it was given the name of 'swing' because of its easy rhythm.

Opposite (bottom)
The mysterious monk, Gregori Rasputin (1871–1916). Widely hated and feared, Rasputin was murdered in 1916.

The jazz trumpeter Louis Armstrong (1900–1971). Born in New Orleans, Armstrong first came to fame in the 1920s with his traditional jazz band 'The Hot Five'. In later life he was still active and recorded popular hits such as 'Mack the Knife' and 'Wonderful World'.

Morton, Duke Ellington and Benny Goodman. They were all American, but people in Europe heard their music on the radio and on the gramophone.

Newspapers and Books

Finally, many people liked to spend their leisure time reading. By the 1930s most children were educated to the age of fourteen or fifteen. Often the teachers were not very good and the children usually misbehaved. However, when they left school, children usually knew how to read and write. So many of them bought newspapers and books to read in their leisure time. Most of the newspapers that we read today were popular in the 1930s. Some people bought them in order to find out the football results and the racing results. Other people bought them to read the political news on the front page. The most popular English newspapers were the *Daily Mirror* and the *Daily Express*. They had plenty of pictures and stories about film-stars and criminals.

All these forms of entertainment helped people to stay happy during the gloomy years of the Great Depression. They helped people to forget their troubles. That, at least, was something to be thankful for.

2 Communism in Russia

In the early days of April 1917 an express train sped across the plains of central Germany heading for the frontiers of Russia. People looked up in surprise as it thundered past. It was a most unusual sight. Its windows were barred and its doors were tightly locked.

That train was certainly no ordinary train. In fact it was carrying an important Russian revolutionary, Vladimir Ilyich Lenin, to Russia. There he was to lead a revolution that was to change the history of the world: the Russian Revolution of 1917. That revolution brought to power the first communist government ever to be seen in Europe.

Tsar Nicholas II

In 1917 Russia was a huge country with over one hundred and fifty million inhabitants. It was ruled by the heavy hand of Tsar Nicholas II. The Tsar was a tyrant. He would not tolerate anyone who opposed his government. Those people who criticised him were promptly put into prison and sent to the frozen wastes of Siberia. Even the Duma (the Russian parliament) did not dare to criticise his actions.

Rasputin

The Tsar's chief adviser was a strange monk, Gregori Rasputin. Rasputin was a tall, black-haired man with a long, straggly beard. In fact he was a hypnotist and had very unusual powers. He had the power to heal the Tsar's young son, Alexei, who suffered from the disease of haemophilia. This gave Rasputin great influence over the Tsar, for without Rasputin the child would surely die.

Rasputin used his influence to make sure that his friends were given important offices in the Tsar's government. They then used these offices to make themselves rich. Most people in Russia hated Rasputin and his friends. So they also grew to dislike his master the Tsar.

Tsar Nicholas II of Russia (1868–1918) with the Crown Prince Alexei.

Peasants and Factory Workers

There were many other reasons why the Russian people came to dislike the Tsar. Most Russians were peasants and they lived in great poverty. They used old-fashioned farming methods which gave them poor yields from their land. Their farms were often too small to supply their own needs and the needs of their families. Many of them owned no land at all. Therefore they had to rent land from the rich nobility, who usually charged a high rent. This made the peasants discontented and angry.

The factory workers were even worse off than the peasants. The Industrial Revolution came to Russia in the late nineteenth century. This was much later than in Britain and the rest of Europe. However, it brought to Russia all the evils of factory work. People were forced to work long hours in return for extremely low wages. They lived in terrible slums and died at a young age from painful diseases. Trade unions were banned by the government. So,

209

like the peasants, the workers had little love for the Tsar and his government. They looked forward to the day when reforms would come to Russia.

Lenin and the Bolsheviks

Yet who would bring about these reforms? Most of the political parties in Russia had been persecuted by Tsar Nicholas II. Therefore they had left the country and gone into exile. The most important of these parties was the Bolshevik Party. The Bolsheviks were followers of the ideas of Karl Marx. They wanted to bring about a socialist revolution in Russia so that power could be given to the workers and peasants. Their leader was a man called Vladimir Ilyich Lenin—the man in the train at the beginning of this chapter.

Lenin was the son of a humble school inspector. When he was sixteen years old his brother was executed for taking part in a plot to overthrow the Tsar. This made Lenin a strong opponent of the Russian government. Soon he read the works of Karl Marx. They convinced him that socialism was the only way to bring justice to Russia. At one stage he was arrested because of his views and sent to prison in Siberia for three years. In 1900 he left Russia and went to live in Germany and Switzerland. There he wrote many pamphlets and books about socialism. All the time he made plans for a socialist revolution in Russia, and waited for a chance to return there.

The Fall of the Tsar

In 1917 Lenin's chance came at last. The First World War had been going on for almost three years. As we saw earlier (in chapter 8) the Russian armies suffered heavy defeats. Hundreds of thousands of men were killed in battle. Many more deserted and refused to fight. All over the country there was a shortage of food. By late 1916 there were long queues outside the food shops. Bread in particular was expensive and difficult to get. Soon workers began to go on strike in protest against these conditions.

In March 1917 there were serious riots in the city of St Petersburg (now

Vladimir Ilyich Lenin (1870–1924): a picture taken in 1900.

Poverty in Tsarist Russia: a village scene.

called Leningrad). Tsar Nicholas II was forced to abdicate and a new govern-ment came to power. This government was led by a lawyer called Alexander Kerensky. Kerensky wanted to introduce reforms that would help the poor. He wanted Russia to be a deomocratic state. However, before this could be done he wanted Russia to defeat Germany in the war. Therefore he ordered the Russian armies to launch a new offensive.

The Bolsheviks opposed this policy. They pointed out that the war brought

A revolutionary meeting in St Petersburg in 1917.

211

misery to the peasants and workers. They wanted Russia to withdraw from the war. Only if there was peace, they claimed, could socialism be introduced into Russia. The German government was interested by this. It decided to help the Bolsheviks seize power in order that Russia would withdraw from the war. This would leave German troops free to fight on the western front.

In April 1917 the German government offered Lenin, the Bolsheviks' leader, a free passage from Switzerland to Russia. The train that took him on this journey was the train that we saw at the beginning of this chapter, thundering towards the borders of Russia.

The October Revolution

Lenin soon succeeded in overthrowing the government of Kerensky. In many factories the workers had set up 'soviets', or workers councils. They wanted a socialist revolution and an end to the war. Lenin quickly gained their support. On 6 November, he organised a revolution in St Petersburg against Kerensky. The revolution succeeded. (It was called the October Revolution, because the Russian calendar was thirteen days behind the calendar used in the rest of Europe.) Lenin now became the new ruler of Russia, and he ruled with the support of the Bolshevik Party and the workers soviets. He promised the people 'Peace, Land and Bread'. 'Peace' with Germany, 'Land' for the peasants and 'Bread' for the workers.

Before Lenin could make any reforms he had first to end the war with

Alexander Kerensky (born in 1881), leader of the provisional government in Russia during the summer of 1917. When Lenin and the Bolsheviks later took over power, Kerensky tried to organise resistance against them, but, when this failed, left the country and settled in the U.S.A.

A scene in the streets of St Petersburg during the October Revolution.

212

Trotsky urging on the troops of the Red Army.

Germany. This he did by the Treaty of Brest-Litovsk which was signed in March 1918. The terms of the treaty were harsh, for Russia lost much of her territory in Europe. But this was the price that Lenin was willing to pay in order to secure peace.

Civil War in Russia (1918–21)

Soon after the peace Lenin faced an even more serious threat. Many people in Russia opposed the Bolshevik seizure of power. Some of them wanted to bring the Tsar back to the throne. Therefore, they recruited 'White' armies to fight against the 'Red' armies of the Bolsheviks. In the spring of 1918 civil war broke out in Russia.

At first the situation was very serious. The White armies were very powerful and controlled large parts of the country. They were given support by Britain and France, who did not want to see a communist government in Russia. Nevertheless, the Red armies fought back. They were led by a man called Leon Trotsky. Trotsky, like Lenin, had been forced to go into exile before the revolution because of his socialist views. In 1917 he returned to Russia and Lenin made him Commissar for War.

For most of the civil war Trotsky had his headquarters in a railway carriage. In this he moved around from one army to another, organising their battles and encouraging the men to fight. He enforced rigid discipline on his troops. Once he had ten per cent of a regiment shot because they threatened to mutiny. Nevertheless, this discipline made the Red armies into an efficient fighting force. By 1921 the civil war was over and the Bolsheviks were in complete command of Russia.

Lenin did not live long after the civil war. In 1923 he suffered a severe stroke. On 21 January 1924 he died.

Lenin photographed a few months before the illness which caused his death.

213

During the Civil War famine hit many parts of Russia and killed many people.

The Rise of Stalin

Many people thought that Trotsky would now take over his position as leader of Russia. However, they reckoned without a small man from Georgia, Joseph Stalin. Stalin was secretary of the Communist Party. He was not as clever as Trotsky, but he was a very good organiser. He was also a ruthless man and would tolerate no opposition to his views. In 1927 he had Trotsky expelled from the Communist Party. Two years later he forced him to leave Russia. Stalin was now the most powerful man in the country. He wanted to do two things: firstly, to make Russia strong, and secondly, to make her into a communist state.

Collective Farming

From 1929 onwards Stalin took steps to reform agriculture. He abolished

Lenin addressing a political meeting in Moscow. On the right hand side of the picture is Trotsky. Many years later, when Stalin had come to power and Trotsky had been disgraced, this photograph was altered so that Trotsky no longer appeared in it. In this way Stalin hoped to make people forget how important a part Trotsky played in the Bolshevik revolution.

Joseph Stalin (1879–1953). The son of a humble cobbler, Stalin grew to be one of the most powerful dictators in history. He was the leader of Russia from 1927 until his death in 1953, and ruled the country with a rod of iron.

most private farms. All farms were taken over by the state and the peasants were forced to work on them. This was called 'collective farming'. Some of the most prosperous peasants, the 'kulaks' objected to this because they lost their land. Stalin showed them no mercy. Many millions were executed and thousands of others were sent to 'labour camps'.

A labour camp in Russia in the 1930s. Prisoners were paid four shillings per month for working eighteen hours per day, seven days per week.

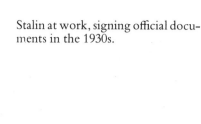
Stalin at work, signing official documents in the 1930s.

Stalin also took steps to strengthen Russia's industries. He drew up a series of 'Five Year Plans' in 1928, 1933 and 1938. These plans built up vital industries such as iron and steel, coal, electricity and oil. All factories were brought under state control and workers were made to work harder than ever before. Stalin's aim was to make Russia into a powerful industrial nation. He quickly succeeded, for soon Russia's industries were second only to those of the United States.

The Great Purge

Stalin also punished anyone who criticised his rule. In 1936 he began a series of political trials which became known as the Great Purge. Many army officers, government ministers and administrators were accused of treason and conspiracy. Thousands of them were executed, and millions more were sent to Siberia to work in labour camps. Some of these people were probably guilty of plotting to overthrow Stalin. However, most of them were people that Stalin wanted to get rid of because they were rivals to his power.

By 1939 communist Russia was a powerful country. Many things had changed since the days of the Tsar. Corruption and poverty were at an end. Every Russian had a roof over his head and sufficient to eat. However, he still had very little freedom. He had to obey the commands of Stalin and the Communist Party. This made Stalin one of the most powerful dictators in Europe.

Benito Mussolini (1883–1945): this picture was taken in 1920, just before he came to power.

Victor Emmanuel III, King of Italy from 1900–46.

3 Fascism in Italy

The rise of communist Russia caused great concern to many people in Europe. They were afraid of communism. They feared that communists would seize power elsewhere in Europe and set up dictatorships as they had in Russia.

In some countries there were clever men who played on these fears. They argued that strong government was needed in order to keep the communists under control. They persuaded people to vote them into power and then they set up their own dictatorships. This happened in Italy with the 'fascist' dictatorship of Benito Mussolini.

Mussolini's Youth

Benito Mussolini was born in the village of Doria in 1883. His father was the local blacksmith and his mother was a schoolmistress. As a young boy Mussolini was quarrelsome and he often became involved in street fights. He was also extremely proud and always liked to have his own way. When he left school he qualified as a teacher but he decided to become a journalist instead.

At this stage in his life Mussolini was a communist. He took part in many strikes and encouraged workers to become interested in the ideas of Karl Marx. However, when the First World War broke out Mussolini changed his mind. The Italian Communist Party wanted Italy to stay out of the war. It argued that war would only bring poverty and destruction to the working class. Mussolini, on the other hand favoured war. He hoped that Italy could gain territory from Austria and so become more powerful than ever before. He therefore left the Communist Party and wrote many articles in favour of the war. Eventually the king of Italy, Victor Emmanuel III, gave way. Italy joined the war on the side of France and Britain. Mussolini was delighted and immediately joined the army.

The Founding of the 'Fascists'

The war did not last long for Mussolini. He was wounded in an explosion and soon had to return home. For a while he hobbled around on crutches boasting of his own bravery. Then, when the war ended, he decided to form his own political party. This he did on 23 March 1919. He called his party the *Fascio di Combattimento* (the Fighting Group). As a symbol for the party he chose a bundle of rods with an axe in the middle. This was the symbol of authority that was used in ancient Rome. By this Mussolini showed the Italians that the Fascists would restore Italy to a position of strength and greatness in the world.

The year 1919 was a troubled one for Italy. Like most other countries she was in a bad state after the war. Food was scarce and prices were high. Many industries had closed down and hundreds of thousands of workers were un-employed. Many of them were interested in the Russian Revolution of 1917. They decided that the time had come for a communist revolution in Italy. Workers soviets were set up in many factories, and communists took over power in many small towns and villages.

Mussolini had become a strong opponent of communism. Therefore he organised small squads of blackshirted fascists to go around beating up well-known communists and breaking up their meetings. Their action was supported by the wealthy industrialists and landowners. They feared that if the communists gained power in Italy, they would lose their factories and their land. Mussolini was also supported by many 'devout' Catholics who were afraid of the 'godless' communists.

Mussolini seizes Power

This support encouraged Mussolini and in 1922 he decided that the time had come to try to seize power. In late October he ordered columns of his black-

Mussolini relaxes just before the March on Rome in October 1922.

'Photographs and films showed Mussolini in commanding poses'— Mussolini making a speech in 1928.

shirts to march on Rome to force king Victor Emmanuel III to appoint a fascist government. The king gave in to the threat and appointed Mussolini as Prime Minister. Mussolini was still in Milan when news of the appointment came through. He had not even had the courage to join his own blackshirts in their march on Rome. Nevertheless he hurried there by express train and took up his new appointment. He was to rule Italy for the next twenty years.

Mussolini the 'Superman'

Once he was in power Mussolini tried to build himself up as a 'superman'. He claimed that he could restore order to Italy and make her a great power once more. In schools children were told of the wonderful things that Mussolini was going to do for Italy. They were taught to chant 'Mussolini is right! Mussolini is right!' Photographs and films showed Mussolini in commanding poses, taking the salute at military parades or working hard at his desk. He also posed for pictures which showed him working in the fields or digging roads. The newspapers and the radio always praised Mussolini and talked of his great achievements. In Rome his office light was even left on all night so that people would think he was working late!

Economic Reforms

All this was clever propaganda, designed to make people support Mussolini. Nevertheless he did get certain things done. Farmers were encouraged to use new agricultural methods in order to grow sufficient grain to feed the whole population. Wasteland was drained and brought under cultivation so that it became useful for farming. Fine new motorways, *autostrada,* were built to link up important cities. New railway lines were also built. Mussolini even boasted that he was the first man to make the Italian railways run on time!

Mussolini at work at his desk: but often the light was left on all night, even when he wasn't there, so that the people in the street outside would believe he was still at work.

Pius XI, pope from 1922–1939. He signed the Lateran Treaty and Concordat with Mussolini.

Mussolini and the Catholic Church

One of his greatest achievements was to end the old quarrel between Italy and the papacy. Ever since 1870 successive popes had refused to recognise the Kingdom of Italy. They claimed that Rome belonged to them, and that it should not have been taken over by Italy (see chapter 4). Mussolini solved this problem. In 1929 he negotiated an agreement with Pope Pius XI called the Lateran Treaty and Concordat. This allowed the pope to be the ruler of the Vatican City in the middle of Rome. It also made Catholicism the state religion of Italy. The pope was pleased with the agreement and said: 'We have given God to Italy and Italy to God'. Catholics all over Europe approved because it solved the old quarrel between Italy and the pope. Mussolini was also pleased, for the agreement gave him prestige and assured him of the loyalty of all Italian Catholics.

Mussolini the Dictator

Despite all these achievements Mussolini was a ruthless dictator. He banned all political parties in Italy except the Fascist Party. The blackshirts were used as a special police force. They arrested people who criticised Mussolini and imprisoned them without trial. Often they beat them up and murdered them. In 1924 a leading socialist Giacomo Matteotti was murdered by a group of fascists. It was two years before they were put on trial and even then they were only lightly punished.

Trade unions were also brought under the control of the government. Workers were made to work long hours and were not allowed to strike for more pay. Young children were forced to join the Fascist Youth (the *Ballila*).

A parade of the Fascist Youth in Rome in 1935.

Mussolini takes the salute.

There they dressed in military uniforms and learnt how to use toy machine guns. Like all other Italians they were told to work hard and to be obedient to their government. So, in his own way, Mussolini established a dictatorship which was every bit as ruthless as the dictatorship of Stalin.

4   Hitler and the Rise of Nazi Germany

The years after the First World War were troubled years for Germany. Her economy had been ruined by the war effort and many industries had been forced to close down. Thousands of workers were unemployed and roamed about the country in search of work. Soldiers, home from the front, were unable to find work either. Food was also scarce and women had to queue for hours to get their rations.

The Weimar Republic (1919–33)

At times such as this people often look to their government for help. After the war had ended elected representatives of the German people had met together in the town of Weimar to draw up a new constitution for their country. They made Germany into a democratic republic known as the Weimar Republic. However, most Germans had no confidence in the Weimar Republic. They resented the fact that they had lost the war. They also disliked the Treaty of Versailles because it had blamed Germany for the war and made her pay compensation to her enemies (see chapter 8). There-fore they criticised the leaders of the Weimar Republic for accepting the treaty. They also blamed them for the unemployment and misery that they

Economic troubles in Germany after the war: in 1923 inflation was so bad in Germany that the government had to print billion mark notes.

223

Unemployed workers march through the streets.

were suffering. One of the strongest critics of the Weimar Republic was a small man with a neat black moustache. That man was Adolf Hitler. He was soon to become the leader of Germany and the most feared man in Europe.

Adolf Hitler's Childhood

Adolf Hitler was born in the small Austrian village of Branau in 1889. His father was a German-Austrian (there were many millions of Germans living in Austria at this time). He worked as a customs official and was well known for his bad temper. Hitler had an unhappy childhood. He disliked his father and he was not very good at school. One of his teachers later said of him 'He lacked self-control and was proud, stubborn, bad-tempered and lazy'.

When he was nineteen years old Hitler left home and went to seek his fortune in Vienna. He wanted to become a painter but few people were interested in buying his paintings. So he quickly ran out of money and had to wander round the streets in shabby second-hand clothes. Sometimes he was so hungry that he joined the beggars who queued outside soup kitchens in order to get something to eat. Often he had to sleep out at night because he could not afford to rent a room.

Hitler and the Jews

It was during this period of his life that Hitler formed his ideas about the Jews. Vienna was a city where there was a lot of anti-semitism (hatred of the Jews).

Children parading with Nazi flags in Munich in 1925.

Many Jews lived there and some of them were very rich. People who were not so well off therefore blamed the Jews for anything that went wrong. They accused Jewish bankers and moneylenders of deliberately starving poor people. They spread stories about the cruel things that Jews did to old people and young children. Most of these stories were completely untrue. However, it was all too easy for poor people to believe them. Hitler was poor and he believed them. He soon became convinced that the Jews were a wicked and dangerous race of people. He was to remain anti-semitic (a hater of Jews) for the rest of his life.

When the First World War broke out Hitler enlisted in the German army. He fought bravely in the trenches in France and was wounded twice. Once he was shot in the leg and another time he was blinded by poison gas. Nevertheless, he recovered and was awarded the medal of the Iron Cross for his bravery.

The Betrayal of Germany

When Germany finally surrendered in 1918 Hitler was bitterly disappointed. By this time he had come to believe that the Germans were a master-race. He thought that the Germans were stronger and more intelligent than any other race in the world. So, in his opinion, Germany's defeat in the war was due to treason. Who had committed this treason? 'The Jews and the communists,'

Adolf Hitler (1889–1945) as a corporal in the First World War.

225

A Nazi torchlight procession.

Joseph Goebbels (1897–1945), one of Hitler's most faithful followers addressing a public meeting in a small German town in 1929. Goebbels was in charge of Nazi propaganda and, when Hitler came to power, was Minister of Propaganda from 1933 to 1945. He died by committing suicide at the end of the Second World War, when it was obvious that Germany would be defeated.

said Hitler. They were the traitors who had betrayed the German people. Therefore Hitler decided to establish a political party in order to rid Germany of traitors and restore her to her former greatness.

The Founding of the Nazi Party

How was it possible to establish a political party? Hitler thought about this carefully and soon saw his chance. In 1919 he was employed by the police to spy on the activities of a small political party, the German Worker's Party. He went along to its meetings to hear what was said there. Then, instead of spying on the party he decided to join it. In 1920 he was elected as its leader and renamed it the National Socialist German Worker's Party. It was soon known as the Nazi party for short.

Hitler quickly built up the strength of the Nazi party. He designed a special party flag with the 'swastika' sign in the middle. He also recruited a private army called the S.A. (stormtroopers). The members of the S.A. wore brown uniforms and carried guns. They kept order at Hitler's meetings and attacked anyone who tried to interrupt him. They also caused trouble at the meetings of Hitler's opponents.

The Munich 'Putsch'

By November 1923 Hitler decided that the time had come for him to seize power. So he organised a revolt in Munich. The revolt started in a beer-hall. 'The National Revolution', shouted Hitler, 'has begun'. However, when Hitler led his stormtroopers to the Munich army barracks, the soldiers opened

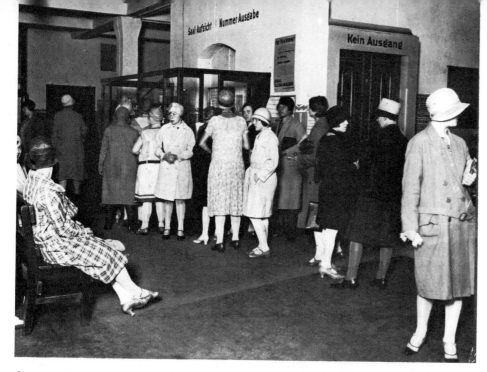

The Great Depression hits Germany: women at a Labour Exchange in 1930 looking for employment.

fire on them. Sixteen stormtroopers were killed and Hitler dislocated his shoulder. The revolt was known as the Munich *putsch* (rebellion). It was a complete failure and Hitler was sentenced to five years in jail as a result.

Hitler only served ten months of his jail sentence. During this time he wrote a book called *Mein Kampf* (My Struggle). It was meant to be the story of his life. However, it turned out to be a long attack on the Jews. It was badly written and full of lies. Most people found it so boring that they gave up reading it after the first few pages. Nevertheless Hitler meant every word that he said. Later on, when he came to power, he put many of the ideas contained in *Mein Kampf* into practice.

Hitler gains Power

When he was released from jail Hitler decided to try to gain power peacefully. He did not have to wait long before his chance came. Earlier in this chapter you read about the terrible economic crisis that swept through Europe in the 1930s. Germany was badly hit by this crisis. Many industries began to close down in 1930, and by 1933 there were over six million people out of work.

In times of crisis people look for a strong leader to give them guidance. The German people looked to Hitler. He blamed Germany's troubles on the Jews and communists. He promised to restore prosperity to Germany and to make her a powerful nation again. People believed him and began to support the Nazi Party. When elections were held in 1932 the Nazi Party

Hitler at a Nazi parade in 1931.

Hitler walking up the steps to the rostrum to deliver a speech at a mass meeting in 1934. This is a good example of the effectiveness of Nazi propaganda; note the huge crowds, the ranks of men in uniform, the swastika arm-bands and the large banners of the SA.

30 January 1933: Hitler shakes hands with President von Hindenburg as he becomes Chancellor.

became the strongest party in the *Reichstag* (the German parliament). In January 1933 President von Hindenburg asked Hitler to become Chancellor and to form a government. Hitler agreed. He was ruler of Germany at last.

The Reichstag Fire

Hitler immediately set about silencing all those who opposed his rule. He was helped in this by a mysterious event. On 27 February 1933 a fire destroyed the buildings in which the *Reichstag* held its meetings. The police immediately arrested a Dutch communist, Martin van der Lubbe, and accused him of starting the fire. He was found guilty and executed. This gave Hitler the chance to claim that the communists were planning to destroy Germany. Everyone believed him and the *Reichstag* voted him full power to rule Germany for a period of four years.

This was exactly what Hitler wanted. Now he began to establish his dictatorship. All political parties, except the Nazi Party, were banned. The newspapers and the radio were censored so that they only gave news that was favourable to Hitler. A special secret police, the *Gestapo*, were established. They imprisoned many leading socialists and trade union leaders. Some of them were tortured and others were executed without trial.

The Hitler Youth on parade.

The 'Night of the Long Knives'

Hitler also took action against some of his own supporters. The leaders of the S.A. (stormtroopers) criticised him for not giving them the top posts in government. Hitler would not tolerate criticism. So, on the night of 30 June 1934 all the leaders of the S.A. were arrested and murdered. This was known as the Night of the Long Knives.

Punching home a point: Hitler addressing a public meeting after taking over power.

Action against the Jews

Hitler was at his most ruthless in his dealings with the Jews. You will remember that he hated the Jews and believed that they had betrayed Germany. Therefore he banned Jews from holding jobs in the civil service or in education. They were also banned from being journalists or taking posts in radio broadcasting. Then in 1935 came the Nuremburg Laws. These deprived Jews of their German citizenship and made it illegal for them to marry non-Jews. Soon many Jews began to leave Germany in order to escape this persecution.

However, there was worse to come. In November 1938 a Jewish boy in Paris shot an official of the German embassy. When the news of this reached Germany, Jewish shops were raided and their windows smashed. Hundreds of Jews were beaten up in the streets and some of them died from their wounds. This was known as the Week of the Broken Glass.

229

People lived in fear of the arrival of the Gestapo trucks, seen here outside a Gestapo building.

Stormtroopers post up notices on the windows of Jewish shops warning people not to buy anything there.

Shortly after this Jews were forbidden to go to cinemas, theatres, schools and universities. Many were arrested and taken off to the concentration camps at Dachau, Buchenwald and Sachsenhausen. There they were locked up, along with communists, socialists and many clergymen who had criticised Hitler. They were starved and made to do forced labour. Many of them were murdered in cold blood.

By 1939 most people in Europe realised what was happening in Germany. They could see that Hitler was a violent and evil dictator. Soon they were to get a chance to fight against that dictatorship, for in 1939 Hitler caused war to break out in Europe. In the next chapter we shall see how he did this.

The railway tracks stretch into the distance towards the terrible concentration camps where Jews were imprisoned and killed.

231

TO DO

1 Pretend that you are the wife of a worker on the dole in the 1930s. Write the diary of a week in your life.

2 Use your Irish history textbook to find out what effect the Great Depression had in Ireland.

3 Which of the following inventions do you think has given people most happiness: the cinema, the television, the radio, the motorcar, or the aeroplane? State the reasons for your choice.

4 Write a short biography of one of the following people: Lenin, Stalin, Mussolini, Hitler. Use an encyclopedia to help you in this.

5 Draw up a list of similarities between Stalin's rule in Russia and Mussolini's rule in Italy. Then draw up a list of the differences. Which of your two lists is the longer?

6 You are a newspaper reporter in Germany during the 1930s. Describe how Hitler came to power. Explain to your readers why the German people supported him and what he did for Germany.

TO READ

Europe, Making the Modern World, John Robottom (ed.), Longman Group.

The Making of Russia, Joan Hasler, Longman Group.

Lenin and the Russian Revolution, Archive Series, F. M. Stacey, Arnold.

Modern Russia, Modern Times, John Robottom, Longman Group.

Lenin and the Russian Revolution, Then and There Series, Donald Mack, Longman Group.

Mussolini and Italy, Modern Times, C. Bayne-Jardine, Longman Group.

Mussolini and the Fascist Era, Archive Series, Desmond Gregory, Arnold.

Bismarck, the Kaiser and Germany, Modern Times, B. J. Elliott, Longman Group.

Hitler and Germany, Modern Times, B. J. Elliott, Longman Group.

Hitler and the Rise of the Nazis, Archive Series, D. M. Phillips, Arnold.

The Russian Revolution, Jackdaw Series no. 42, Jackdaw Publications.

Lenin, Jackdaw Series no. 113, Jackdaw Publications.

DATELINE

1917 The October Revolution in Russia.

1919 Mussolini founds the Fascist Party in Italy.

1920 Hitler founds the Nazi Party in Germany.

1921 End of the civil war in Russia.

1922 Mussolini comes to power in Italy.

First radio broadcasts by the B.B.C.

'Germans beware! Do not buy from Jews!'

1923   The failure of Hitler's Munich *putsch*.
1924   The death of Lenin.
1927   The first talkie film is made.
1929   The Wall Street Crash.
        Trotsky expelled from Russia.
        Mussolini negotiates the Concordat with the pope.
1933   Hitler comes to power in Germany.
1934   The Night of the Long Knives—Hitler murders his opponents.
1936   The beginning of the Great Purge in Russia.
        The Jarrow Hunger March.
        First television broadcasts by the B.B.C.

10   The Second World War, 1939–45

Adolph Hitler was a violent and ambitious man. He wanted to make Germany the most powerful country in Europe. In order to do this, he invaded other countries and took them over by force. This eventually caused war to break out in Europe in 1939. The Second World War was even more terrible than the First World War. It lasted longer, it killed more people and it caused more destruction. The Nazis also carried out some of the worst crimes in the history of the human race.

In this chapter you will see how Hitler caused the Second World War. You will also read about the major battles of the war and see how Germany was finally defeated.

The Second World War was even more terrible than the First World War.

1 The Causes of the War

Adolf Hitler meant every word he had written in *Mein Kampf*.

Hitler had two main aims in his foreign policy. His first aim was to unite all German-speaking people into one single country. Most of them, it is true, already lived in Germany. However, there were also many German-speakers in Poland, Czechoslovakia and Austria. Hitler now wanted to bring these people under the control of Germany. He regarded the Germans as a master-race in Europe, superior to all others. Once they were united he thought that they could dominate the world.

Hitler's other aim was to win more living-space for Germany. He believed that the Treaty of Versailles (1919) had robbed Germany of much of her territory. Therefore he wanted Germany to have parts of Czechoslovakia, Poland, and Russia. This would give the German people more farmland for growing foodstuffs and raw materials for vital industries. In fact it would give the master-race more living-space.

Hitler had written about both these ambitions in his book *Mein Kampf*. He repeated them often in his public speeches. Yet no politician in Europe

235

German troops march into the Rhineland, March 1936.

took him seriously. In Britain and France people thought that he was merely boasting. After the horrors of the First World War they did not want to see war break out again. Therefore they took no action against Hitler until it was almost too late. This was a serious mistake, for Hitler meant every word that he said about winning new living-space for Germany.

Germany re-arms
As soon as he came to power Hitler took steps to build up Germany's strength.

In 1933 he withdrew Germany from the League of Nations and from the disarmament talks that were taking place there. Then he began to increase the size of the German army to five hundred thousand men. By the terms of the Treaty of Versailles this was illegal. The German army should not have contained more than one hundred thousand men. Nevertheless Britain and France did not try to stop Hitler. Soon he was spending huge amounts of money on new arms and equipment.

Invasion of the Rhineland (1936)

Hitler now waited for a chance to test his strength. In October 1935 Mussolini invaded the territory of Abyssinia in East Africa. He did this in order to increase Italy's prestige and to strengthen the Italian Empire in Africa. The League of Nations condemned the invasion and called on all countries to stop trading with Italy. This had no effect. By the spring of 1936 Italy was in complete control of Abyssinia.

Hitler watched all this with great interest. He saw that the League of Nations was unable to stop Italian aggression. So he decided to try some aggression of his own. Under the terms of the Treaty of Versailles Germany was not allowed to station troops within fifty kilometres of the Rhine. This area was known as the 'demilitarised zone'. It meant that if war broke out between France and Germany, France would have an immediate advantage.

Hitler decided that this was intolerable. So on 7 March 1936 he ordered German troops to occupy the demilitarised zone. Secretly he ordered them to retreat if the French army tried to stop them. However, France did nothing and the whole operation was a complete success. Hitler learnt from this that aggression could pay.

The 'Rome–Berlin Axis' (1936)

After the occupation of the Rhineland, Hitler decided to strengthen his position by negotiating an alliance with Mussolini. Both men had a great deal in common. Both men were dictators and despised democracy. Both of them believed in using violence to get what they wanted. Both also wanted to make their countries more powerful. So in October 1936 they signed a secret agreement in which they promised to work together in foreign affairs. This was known as the Rome–Berlin Axis. A month later Hitler signed an agreement with Japan called the Anti-Comintern Pact. By this both countries agreed to work together to stop the spread of communism in the world.

This gave Hitler two powerful allies. Both allies later fought on the side of Germany in the Second World War. The two agreements also gave him the confidence to press on with his plans to create living-space for Germany.

Benito Mussolini and Adolf Hitler signed a secret agreement in October 1936.

In 1936 civil war broke out in
Spain. Hitler supported General
Franco, another dictator, seen here
saluting his followers. Franco was
victorious and still rules in Spain.

Spanish government forces in action
against the Fascist rebels.

238

A street in Madrid during an air-raid. German planes and pilots, sent by Hitler to support Franco, gained experience which they put to good use in the Second World War.

In April 1937 the small Spanish town of Guernica was totally devastated in an unexpected and all-out bombing attack by Heinkel and Stuka bombers. Influenced by this terrifying act, Pablo Picasso, the famous Spanish artist, painted *La Guernica* in which he expressed his protest against the terror and horror of war.

239

'Anschluss' with Austria (1938)

His first target was Austria. In Austria there were seven million German-speaking people. Many of them wanted *Anschluss* (union with Germany). They even formed their own Nazi party which kept in close touch with Hitler. In February 1938 Hitler made his first move. He summoned the Chancellor of Austria, Doctor Kurt von Schuschnigg, to a meeting in his mountain castle at Berchtesgaden. There he demanded that the Austrian Nazis should be allowed to have a say in the government of Austria.

Schuschnigg agreed to this demand. However, he realised that Hitler was planning to take over Austria completely. So when he got back to Vienna he announced that he would hold a referendum on whether Austria should remain independent or be united with Germany. When Hitler heard of this plan he flew into a rage. He was afraid that the Austrians might vote to remain independent. So on 12 March 1938 he sent the German armies into Austria and united Austria with Germany. The *Anschluss* was completed.

A few days later Hitler rode in triumph through the streets of Vienna waving at the cheering crowds. As he did so he must have smiled to himself. Only twenty-five years before he had been a penniless painter in the same city. Now he was a powerful dictator.

The Problem of the Sudetenland

Hitler now turned his attention to Czechoslovakia. Czechoslovakia had been established at the end of the First World War. It contained about fifteen million people. About eight million of them were Czech, three million were Slovaks, and over three million were German speakers. All the German speakers lived in northern Czechoslovakia, in an area known as the Sudetenland. Like the German speakers in Austria they too wanted to be united with Germany.

Hitler decided to take advantage of this. He accused Czechoslovakia of persecuting the Sudeten Germans and demanded that they should be allowed to unite with Germany. The Czech government refused to agree to such a demand and Hitler made preparations for war.

Britain and France were alarmed by this, for they were both allied to Czechoslovakia. If Hitler attacked, they would have to go to Czechoslovakia's defence. Neville Chamberlain, the Prime Minister of Britain, wanted to avoid war at all costs. He therefore decided on a policy of appeasement (keeping the peace). He believed that if Hitler was allowed to take over the Sudetenland, he would make no more demands for territory in Europe. Therefore he called for a conference of the major European powers to discuss Hitler's demand.

Neville Chamberlain, returning from the Munich Conference, spoke of 'peace in our time'.

The Munich Conference

The conference took place in Munich in September 1938. Hitler, Mussolini, Chamberlain and Daladier (for France) were present. They decided that Czechoslovakia should hand over the Sudetenland to Germany. Hitler then promised that he wanted no more territory in Europe. Everyone, except the poor Czechoslovakian government, thought that this was the best solution. Chamberlain was particularly pleased. He thought that his policy of appeasement had worked.

The Invasion of Czechoslovakia (1939)

However, within a few months Hitler showed that he wanted more than just the Sudetenland. He wanted to conquer Czechoslovakia completely, in order to take over the rich Czech industries and to create more living-room for the German people. So, in the early months of 1939 he began to mass troops on the Czechoslovak border ready for an invasion. On 15 March the President of Czechoslovakia went to Berlin in a bid to prevent war. However, Hitler told him that the German armies would invade his country on the next day. If the Czech people resisted, Hitler warned, Prague would be bombed to the ground. The Czech President saw that there was no hope. He told his people not to resist the German invasion and within hours the

German expansion, 1933–39.

Joseph Stalin signed a non-aggression pact with Germany, August 1939.

NORTH SEA

BALTIC SEA

Koningsberg

Danzig

Hamburg

Amsterdam

NETHERLANDS

Berlin

Poznan

Warsaw

BELGIUM

Brussels

Cologne

Leipzig

P O L A N D

LUX.

Frankfurt

Breslau

Rhine River

Cracow

F R A N C E

G E R M A N Y

Prague

BOHEMIA

C Z E C H O

Munich

MORAVIA

S L O V A K I A

Berne

Vienna

Bratislava

SWITZERLAND

A U S T R I A

H U N G A R Y

ROUMANIA

I T A L Y

| Germany 1933 | Rhineland remilitarised 1936 | Annexed 1938 | Annexed 1939 |

German tanks had crossed the border. Czechoslovakia was soon completely taken over by Germany.

The Road to War

Britain and France now realised that Hitler could no longer be trusted. They also realised that his next target would be Poland. By the Treaty of Versailles Poland had been given a strip of land which cut Germany off from her territories in East Prussia. This land was known as the Polish Corridor, because it gave Poland an outlet to the sea. In the summer of 1939 Hitler made it clear that he wanted to take over the Polish Corridor and that he would invade Poland to do so. Britain and France therefore made a solemn promise to Poland that they would come to her aid if Hitler launched an attack.

This did not worry Hitler very much. He knew that Britain and France were too far away to give Poland much help. Instead he worried about the attitude of Stalin and the Russian government. Russia shared frontiers with Poland and did not want to see her taken over by Germany. Stalin also disliked Hitler and condemned everything that the Nazis stood for. Therefore he tried to persuade Britain and France to join him in a war against Germany.

The British government refused to do this because it distrusted Stalin and disliked communism. So Stalin, realising that Russia could not fight Germany alone, decided to join with Hitler rather than oppose him. On 23 August 1939 Russia and Germany signed a non-aggression pact. In this they agreed not to go to war with each other. They also agreed to divide Poland between themselves.

Hitler now knew that he could invade Poland without the risk of a war with Russia. On 1 September German tanks rumbled over the Polish frontier and the invasion was on. Two days later Britain and France honoured their promise to Poland by declaring war on Germany. The Second World War had begun.

Hitler announces the invasion of Poland in the Reichstag, September 1939.

A Stuka dive-bomber of the German Luftwaffe in action.

2 'Blitzkrieg' in Europe

As you saw in the last section, the Second World War began when Germany invaded Poland. In this invasion the German armies used a special method of attack which came to be known as *blitzkrieg* (shock warfare).

The 'Blitzkrieg'

The blitzkrieg usually began just before dawn. The *Luftwaffe* (German Air Force) attacked the enemy's airfields and bombed bridges, railway lines and army headquarters. This destroyed the enemy's air defences and ruined his communications. Then, a few hours later, the *Panzer* (tank) divisions swept forward and smashed through the enemy lines. Often they surrounded the enemy with a great 'pincer' movement so that no troops could escape. The infantry then followed up in their jeeps, lorries and motor cars. They dealt with the troops and finished off any pockets of resistance. The whole operation was done at high speed and this gave it the name *blitzkrieg*.

Opposite (top)
Poland provided poor resistance for German guns and tanks.

Opposite (bottom)
German troops invade Poland.

244

An 'armada' of ships large and small, under constant attack, rescued large numbers of troops from Dunkirk.

The Invasion of France

The German armies had quickly conquered Poland by the end of September 1939. Hitler then turned his attention towards France and the Low Countries (Holland and Belgium). On 9 May 1940 his armies swept into Belgium and Holland. Six days later they invaded France. Britain came to the aid of France but the French and British armies could find no answer to the *blitzkrieg* tactics. They were forced to retreat and soon found themselves trapped in northern France, surrounded on all sides by the German armies. There was only one possible way for them to escape: through the port of Dunkirk and across the channel to England. If that failed, then everyone knew that they would be killed or taken prisoner.

Rescue at Dunkirk

When news of this desperate situation reached Britain, urgent appeals were broadcast over the radio. Everyone who owned a boat was asked to cross the channel to Dunkirk and rescue the trapped troops. Immediately hundreds of boats set sail from the ports of south and east England. They looked a strange sight—pleasure steamers, fishing vessels, motor boats, yachts and even rowing boats. Yet between 27 May and 4 June they took three hundred and thirty thousand troops from the beaches of Dunkirk to safety in England. This was a great rescue operation.

Not all escaped in the evacuation of Dunkirk.

Exhausted troops return home from Dunkirk.

Those who could afford to fled from Paris in September 1939 to avoid possible bombing.

German troops enter Paris.

A TOUS LES FRANÇAIS

La France a perdu une bataille!
Mais la France n'a pas perdu la guerre!

Des gouvernants de rencontre ont pu capituler, cédant à la panique, oubliant l'honneur, livrant le pays à la servitude. Cependant, rien n'est perdu!

Rien n'est perdu, parce que cette guerre est une guerre mondiale. Dans l'univers libre, des forces immenses n'ont pas encore donné. Un jour, ces forces écraseront l'ennemi. Il faut que la France, ce jour-là, soit présente à la victoire. Alors, elle retrouvera sa liberté et sa grandeur. Tel est mon but, mon seul but!

Voilà pourquoi je convie tous les Français, où qu'ils se trouvent, à s'unir à moi dans l'action, dans le sacrifice et dans l'espérance.

Notre patrie est en péril de mort.
Luttons tous pour la sauver!

VIVE LA FRANCE!

J. de Gaulle

JUIN 1940   GÉNÉRAL DE GAULLE

On 18 June 1940, shortly before France surrendered, General Charles de Gaulle flew to England and appealed to Frenchmen to join him in carrying on the fight against Germany. In London he established the 'Free France' movement which many Frenchmen left their country to join. When France was liberated in 1944 he became its leader for a short time, and was President of France from 1959 to 1969.

The escape from Dunkirk did not stop Hitler conquering France. On 14 June the German armies marched into Paris and a few days later the French government surrendered. Just before this surrender Mussolini had joined the war on Hitler's side. To many people it seemed that Germany was now unbeatable.

The Battle of Britain

Hitler's next aim was to defeat Britain. He decided that the best way of doing this was to first destroy the R.A.F. (Royal Air Force). Then the German armies would be able to cross the channel safely and overrun the country. In July 1940 the Luftwaffe began to bomb towns in the south of England. Then, in early August, the 'Battle of Britain' really started. Hundreds of German *Messerschmitts* flew in over airfields in Britain in an all-out attack on the R.A.F. The R.A.F. fought back with their Spitfires and Hurricanes. For the next five weeks the skies over Britain were filled with battling planes. Hundreds of them were shot down in flames. Many more were badly damaged and had to return to base. By late September the Luftwaffe realised that it could not win. It had already lost over seventeen hundred planes. So Hitler reluctantly called off the attack and postponed his plans to conquer Britain.

During the winter of 1940 German planes continued to bomb London and other important cities. The R.A.F. hit back by carrying out bombing raids against German war industries. This bombing caused a good deal of damage in both countries. Whole cities were destroyed, factories were flattened and many people killed. However, neither side was able to damage the other sufficiently to win the war.

Hitler invades Russia

Hitler did not worry too much over his failure to invade Britain. Already he was dreaming of further conquests. Despite his alliance with Stalin in 1939, he had always intended to invade Russia. Russia contained the living-space that Hitler wanted for the German people. She had valuable raw materials and powerful industries that Germany needed for the war effort. She was also a communist country and Hitler hated communism. So he planned to invade Russia as far as the Ural mountains. When he had done this he could starve most Russians to death and deport the rest to Siberia. They would then be replaced by Germans and the whole area would be annexed to Germany. This, Hitler believed, would give the master-race its living-space.

Messerschmitt fighter planes of the
Luftwaffe.

A wrecked German bomber under
guard.

British pilots 'scramble' to their
Hurricanes.

251

Spitfires in flight.

Bomb damage to British cities was severe in 1940.

The Russian winter caused problems for Hitler's army as it had for Napoleon's.

German Victories in Russia

Throughout the spring of 1941 Hitler made careful preparations for the invasion of Russia. Then, on 22 June the invasion began. Ten thousand tanks and three million soldiers poured into Russia. Overhead the Luftwaffe swooped over the Russian airfields and destroyed hundreds of aircraft before they could leave the ground. Once again the *blitzkrieg* was successful and the Russian armies were caught by surprise. They were forced to retreat and lost many men both killed and wounded. In the city of Kiev seven hundred thousand Russian troops were surrounded and forced to surrender. By December the German armies had advanced six hundred miles and were close to Moscow. Hitler said proudly, 'The enemy is already broken and will never rise again'.

The German Armies run into Problems

However, the situation was not really as good as Hitler thought. One problem was the Russian railway system. This had broad-gauge lines which were useless for the German locomotives and trucks. As they advanced into Russia, the Germans had to rebuild every inch of railway line so that guns, ammunition and clothing could be transported to their armies. This slowed down the German advance and meant that the troops were often short of supplies.

Another problem was the Russian winter. If you remember, Napoleon had been caught out by this. He had lost many thousands of troops in 1812

An anti-Russian poster issued by the Germans in France.

253

Arms and supplies were sent in convoy to Russia, many ships were sunk.

during his slow retreat from Moscow (see chapter 3). If Hitler had listened to his teachers at school he might have heard of this. He might even have learnt from Napoleon's mistake. However, he did not, and the German armies were soon in trouble.

The Russian winter of 1941–42 was a very hard one. Snow began to fall in October and the roads became a sea of mud. As the temperature dropped below freezing point, the oil in the lorries and tanks began to freeze. Men had to light fires under them to get them started, but some of them were completely ruined and had to be left behind. The troops suffered worst of all. No one had thought of giving them suitable clothing for the Russian winter. Soon many of them began to get frostbite and pneumonia. They huddled round fires in a desperate attempt to keep warm. Some of them even ripped clothes from the dead bodies of Russian soldiers, because at least the Russians were well clothed for their own winter.

Pearl Harbour
Despite all these problems Hitler was in a strong position by the end of 1941.

Furthest extent of Axis power

Extent of German and Italian power in 1941.

His armies commanded nearly the whole of Europe: from France to Russia and from Denmark to Greece. With his ally Mussolini, he had also conquered large parts of north Africa.

Field Marshal Rommel, the German commander, had been successful in north Africa. Short of supplies and out-manoeuvred he was finally defeated.

Then, in December 1941, something happened that changed the whole course of the war. In the Far East Japan was anxious to increase her power. In order to do this she had to attack the United States of America, which controlled many islands in the Pacific Ocean. So in the early morning of 7 December the Japanese air force bombed the United States fleet, anchored in Pearl Harbour. Over one hundred planes swooped down from the early morning clouds and dropped their bombs with deadly accuracy. They sank nineteen ships, destroyed one hundred and twenty aircraft and killed over two thousand men.

Hitler declares war on the United States

Germany and Italy were both allies of Japan. So, on 11 December, both countries also declared war on the United States. By doing this they changed

Early on a Sunday morning in December 1941 Japanese bombers attack Pearl Harbour.

256

Pearl Harbour: American planes destroyed on the ground.

the whole course of the war. From now on the United States fought along-side Britain and Russia against Hitler. Once before, during the First World War, the United States had helped to defeat Germany. Soon she was to do so again. Many people think that when Hitler declared war on the United States he made the biggest mistake of his whole career.

3 The Defeat of Hitler

From 1942 onwards most people realised that Hitler could not win the war. They knew that he could not defeat the combined strength of the United States, Russia and Britain. However, Hitler refused to believe this. He was certain that Germany could not be beaten and he was determined to fight to the bitter end.

The Battle of Stalingrad

In the summer of 1942 Hitler pressed on with his invasion of Russia. Most of Russia's oil supplies came from the region of Baku near the Caspian Sea. They were transported up the river Volga to Stalingrad and then distributed to the rest of Russia. Hitler therefore decided to capture Stalingrad so that he could cut off these supplies and force Russia to surrender.

In September 1942 the German armies launched their attack on Stalingrad. The Russians fought back desperately so that the Germans had to fight their way into the city house by house. Then in November three Russian armies under the command of General Zhukov suddenly surrounded Stalingrad. They trapped two hundred and fifty thousand German troops inside the

In freezing conditions, German troops at Stalingrad man their guns.

In almost every country occupied by the Germans a resistance group was set up. Marshal Tito of Yugoslavia played an important part in his country's resistance.

city and gave them no chance of retreat. Throughout December and January the Germans stayed in the city. Many of them froze to death in the bitterly cold weather. Others died from hunger as their food supplies ran out. Finally on 31 January 1943 they surrendered. Out of the original two hundred and fifty thousand men, there were only ninety thousand left. It was a great defeat for Hitler and soon the German armies were forced to retreat slowly from Russia.

The Invasion of Italy

Hitler soon suffered another setback—this time in Italy. In July 1943 British and American troops landed in Sicily. They quickly conquered the island and crossed to the mainland to begin an invasion of Italy. When news of this invasion reached Rome there was a revolt against Mussolini. The king dismissed him from office and had him put under arrest. Then on 3 December, the king signed a truce with the United States and Britain which took Italy out of the war.

Hitler was stunned when he heard this news. He called Italy's surrender: 'a gigantic example of swinishness'. He decided that, if the Italians would not fight then the Germans would fight for them. German paratroopers rescued Mussolini from jail while German armies moved to the south of

A German train after attack by members of the French resistance fighters *(Maquis)*.

German soldiers and civilians during a break in an allied bombing attack on a German city, 1943.

Italy to resist the British and American invasion. They defended strongly but were slowly forced to retreat. On 4 June 1944 American troops entered Rome. Hitler now realised that he had lost control of Italy.

D-Day for Europe (6 June 1944)

Only two days after Rome was captured, Hitler received news of an even worse setback. For some time Britain and the United States had been planning an invasion of France. This would make it possible for them to invade Germany and to link up with the Russian armies which were advancing across eastern Europe. In 1944 they finally agreed on a plan. Normandy was chosen as the area for the invasion. It was close to Britain and had good beaches so that men could be landed easily. The invasion was given the name Operation Overlord and D-Day (Deliverance Day) was fixed for early June. During the spring of 1944 over two million British and American troops were moved to southern England, ready for action.

The Germans knew that an invasion was being planned. However, they expected it to come further up the coast, at Calais. Therefore they moved their strongest forces there and left Normandy only lightly protected.

On 6 June 1944 D-Day arrived and the invasion started. In the early hours of the morning two thousand bombers pounded the German defensive

Two men who played an important part in the defeat of Hitler: Winston Churchill, the British Prime Minister, and the British soldier General Montgomery.

Opposite (bottom)
Allied troops land in Normandy, 7 June 1944.

Allied soldiers advance from the Normandy beach-head.

French Forces of the Interior round up German prisoners.

General de Gaulle, leader of the Free French forces.

positions in Normandy. Then, at 6.30 a.m., the first troops began to wade ashore from the landing craft that had brought them from England. They had to brave the dangers of underwater mines, barbed wire barricades and enemy gunfire. Nevertheless most of them survived and reached the beaches. Within a week three hundred thousand troops had landed in Normandy and the invasion of France was in full swing. Six months later France and Belgium had been liberated from German rule. Everything was now ready for the final invasion.

Hitler commits suicide

Most people now realised that Germany could not avoid defeat. However, Hitler refused to believe it. He ordered his armies to fight to the death and not to surrender. For most of the war he had lived in East Prussia, in an underground bunker called the Wolf's Lair. By January 1945 he could no longer stay there. The Russian armies were preparing to invade Germany from the east and the British and Americans from the west. So Hitler moved to Berlin and fixed his headquarters in an underground bunker near the Chancellery building. He was now a very sick man. Years of hard work had made him look very old. He needed drugs to keep him going throughout the day. His hands trembled and his eyes twitched nervously. He lost his temper more easily than ever before and accused all his colleagues of betraying him. The only person that he trusted was his mistress, Eva Braun. He had known her for many years and she stayed with him to the end.

By late April 1945 even Hitler realised that all was lost. Russian troops surrounded Berlin, and the British and Americans were not far away. On

On 26 April 1945 American and Russian soldiers meet in the town of Torgau, seventy-five miles south of Berlin.

The Japanese town of Hiroshima after the atomic bomb attack.

29 April he married Eva Braun. Then, on the afternoon of the next day he asked his companions to leave the two of them alone together in a small room. There he shot himself while Eva Braun took poison. Their bodies were then taken outside, soaked in petrol and set alight. Within two hours all that was left was a heap of charred bones. On 7 May Germany finally surrendered.

The Atomic Bomb defeats Japan

The war was not yet over. In the Far East Hitler's ally, Japan, continued to fight. By the summer of 1945 everybody could see that she would be defeated. Yet her rulers refused to surrender. So the United States and Britain decided to use a new and terrible weapon that their scientists had just invented: the atomic bomb.

263

Women in the concentration camp at Auschwitz.

The ovens where the bodies of men, women and children, who had been gassed to death, were burned.

On 6 August 1945 an American B29 bomber, nicknamed Enola Gray, dropped the first atomic bomb on the city of Hiroshima. On 9 August another was dropped on the city of Nagasaki. Both bombs caused terrible damage. They exploded with a deafening roar and sent a mushroom of smoke for miles into the sky. They flattened all the buildings in both cities and started raging fires. Over one hundred and sixty thousand people were killed outright. Most of them were innocent women and children who had taken no part in the war. Thousands more died later from the effects of radioactivity that the bombs had left in the air. People are still dying today from the effects of that radioactivity.

The Japanese leaders quickly realised that they had no answer to the atomic bomb. On 14 August they surrendered. The war was over. The world was at peace at last.

The Horrors of War

In 1945 Europe lay in ruins. Thousands of houses had been destroyed and whole cities had been bombed to the ground. Fifty million people had died as a result of the fighting all over the world. Thirty million of these died in Europe and over half of them were ordinary civilians.

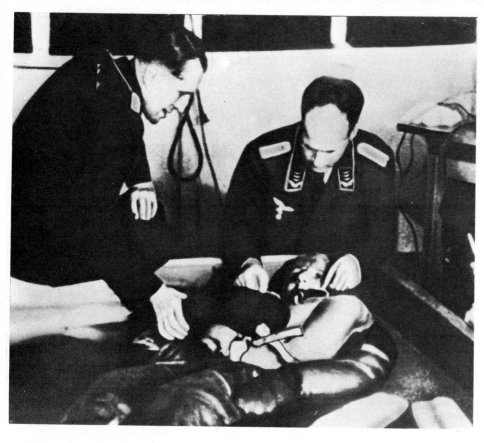

A medical experiment is carried out on a prisoner in the Dachau concentration camp.

The Jews had suffered most of all. You will remember that Hitler had persecuted the German Jews before the outbreak of the war. During the war his armies captured large numbers of them in the countries that they conquered. In 1942 Hitler decided to put into effect his 'final solution': the murder of all Jews in Europe.

All the Jews under German rule were arrested and put into concentration camps. Many of them died from starvation or disease. Others were shot. The rest were gassed to death in special gas chambers in the concentration camps of Auschwitz, Buchenwald, Belsen and Treblinka. Almost six million Jews were murdered in this way.

Germany Divided

The task of settling the peace was carried out by the three victorious allies: the United States, Britain and Russia. They decided that Germany would be divided into four zones. Three of the zones were to be governed by them-

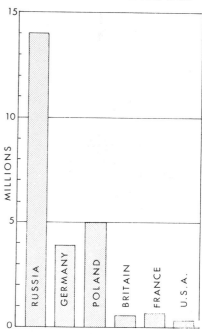

Deaths in the Second World War.

The German city of Dresden in
1945.

selves and the fourth was to be governed by France. The city of Berlin, which lay in the Russian zone, was also divided into four parts in the same way. This was intended to be a temporary arrangement until a more permanent peace treaty could be worked out. However, it lasted for many years after 1945.

The United Nations

The allies also agreed to set up a new world organisation to keep the peace. You will remember that the League of Nations had been set up in 1919 after the First World War. However, this had failed to prevent war in 1939. So in the summer of 1945 an international conference was held at San Francisco in the United States. This set up the United Nations Organisation with its headquarters at New York. The United Nations was similar to the League of Nations but it was much more efficient because more countries joined it.

Symbol of the United Nations.

Headquarters of the United Nations, New York.

Joachim von Ribbentrop.

Kaltenbrunner.

The Nuremburg Trials

Finally the allied powers decided that certain German politicians and generals should be punished for their activity during the war. They were accused of causing the outbreak of war in 1939 and of 'committing crimes against humanity'. The most famous trials took place at Nuremburg in 1946. Twenty-one leading Nazis were tried there. Eleven of them were sentenced to death and seven of them were given long prison sentences. Among those who were executed were von Ribbentrop (Hitler's Foreign Minister) and Kaltenbrunner (the chief of the *Gestapo*). Hermann Göring, another of Hitler's close associates, was also sentenced to death. However, two hours before the time fixed for his execution, he swallowed cyanide that had been smuggled into his cell. He died immediately.

Some Comments

The defeat of Nazi Germany was a great achievement. It saved Europe from the domination of Adolf Hitler, the most evil ruler of modern times. Nevertheless this had only been achieved at a great cost. Europe in 1945 was a poor and devastated continent. No longer was it the most rich and powerful continent in the world. From 1945 onwards it was overshadowed by two new giants: the United States and Russia.

TO DO

1 In your opinion what was the most important battle of the Second World War? Give reasons for your choice.
2 Try to find out what the following people did during the war: Winston Churchill, Charles de Gaulle, General Eisenhower, Field-Marshal Montgomery, Joseph Stalin. Use an encyclopedia and other history books to help you in this.
3 What were the main mistakes that Hitler made during the course of the war? Which of them was the most important?
4 Try to find out more about the aeroplanes that were used during the war. Compare them with those that were used during the First World War.
5 Why did more people die in the Second World War than in the First World War?
6 Compare the map of Europe in 1945 with that of 1919. Draw up a list of the major differences.
7 Try to find out more about the United Nations Organisation and the work that it does in the world today.
8 How did the Second World War affect Ireland?

TO READ

The League of Nations and U.N.O., Modern Times, S. R. Gibbons and P. Morican, Longman Group.
Europe, Making the Modern World, John Robottom (ed.), Longman Group.
World War Two, Modern Times, C. Bayne-Jardine, Longman Group.
The Coming of War, Jackdaw Series no. 64, Jackdaw Publications.
Battle of Britain, Jackdaw Series no. 65, Jackdaw Publications.
Britain at War, Jackdaw Series no. 66, Jackdaw Publications.
The United Nations, Jackdaw Series no. 100, Jackdaw Publications.

DATELINE

1933 Germany withdraws from the League of Nations.
1935 Italy invades Abyssinia.
1936 Germany moves troops into the demilitarised zone of the Rhineland.
1938 March: the *Anschluss* with Austria.
     September: the Munich conference—Sudetenland given to Germany.
1939 March: German troops move into Czechoslovakia.
     August: non-aggression pact between Russia and Germany.
     September: Germany invades Poland—the Second World War begins.
1940 June: Germany defeats France.
     August-September: the Battle of Britain.
1941 June: Germany invades Russia.
     December: Pearl Harbour—United States joins the war.
1942 November: the Battle of Stalingrad begins.
1943 July: allied invasion of Italy.
1944 June: D-Day—allied invasion of France.
1945 April: Hitler commits suicide.
     May: Germany surrenders.
     August: atomic bombs dropped on Hiroshima and Nagasaki—Japan surrenders.

Hermann Göring.

A German family experiences the terror of war, 1944.

269

11 Europe Since the Second World War

Many years have now passed since the end of the Second World War. During these years Europe has changed in many ways. Hundreds of fine cities which were ruined during the war have been rebuilt. Many leading statesmen have retired or died. A whole new generation of people have been born—including yourselves—with new attitudes towards life.

While all this has been going on, two important developments have taken place. Firstly Europe has become less important in the world. She has become involved in the rivalry between the United States and Russia, the so-called cold war. Secondly the countries in western Europe have learnt to co-operate with one another in political and economic affairs. This has resulted in a long period of peace and prosperity. You will read about these important developments in this chapter.

In 1945 Berliners were digging potatoes in front of the shattered Reichstag where Hitler had announced the war in 1939.

1 The 'Cold War'

In 1945 many people hoped that the United States, Britain and Russia would work together to rebuild Europe. However, this was not to be. Instead a 'cold war' developed between the United States and Russia. The cold war divided Europe into two rival groups of countries.

Disagreements between United States and Russia

During the war against Hitler the Russian armies had advanced across eastern Europe into Germany. When the war ended many governments in western Europe began to distrust Stalin. They feared that he might use his powerful armies to make more conquests in western Europe. The President of the United States, Harry Truman, was also afraid of this. He was strongly anti-communist and was determined to make sure that Russia did not gain any more territory in Europe.

Stalin, on the other hand, was afraid of the power of the United States. He knew that both the United States and Britain possessed atomic bombs. He

Hundreds of fine cities that were destroyed during the war have since been rebuilt—a view of modern Berlin.

Russian leader Stalin (left) with American President Truman.

feared that they might use them on Russia in order to rid the world of communism. Therefore he began to tighten his grip on the small countries of eastern Europe. By 1948 there were communist governments in Bulgaria, Rumania, Albania, Poland, Hungary and Czechoslovakia. All of them obeyed Stalin's wishes and were completely loyal to him.

The Berlin Blockade

In 1948 the cold war took a turn for the worst. You will remember that when the war ended, Berlin (which was in the Russian occupied zone of Germany) was divided up between the four major powers. Russia governed east Berlin. The United States, Britain and France governed west Berlin. Stalin soon became worried by the fact that many people from east Germany were using west Berlin as an escape route to west Germany. By 1948 thousands of east Germans had escaped from Russian rule in this way. In June 1948 Stalin imposed a blockade on west Berlin. He cut off all the road and rail connec-

Cold War Europe.

Communist bloc | Communist but neutral | N.A.T.O. Countries | The 'Iron Curtain'

tions between Berlin and west Germany. He hoped that this would force the western powers to pull out of west Berlin altogether.

At first everyone wondered what the western powers would do. Would they do as Stalin wished and pull out of Berlin? Would they try to force their way overland to Berlin? Would they go to war with Russia and start a Third World War? Nobody really knew.

'Operation Vittles'. Watched by anxious Berliners, an American superfortress plane flies in supplies to west Berlin.

In fact the western powers made a bold decision. They decided to break the blockade by organising an airlift of all essential supplies to Berlin. In this way they could keep in contact with the city without risking a war with Russia. The airlift was called Operation Vittles. Every day huge transport planes took off from airports in west Germany, loaded with food and clothing. Soon four thousand tons of supplies were being flown into west Berlin each day. This eventually persuaded Stalin that the blockade would not work. So on 11 May 1949 he called it off and re-opened the rail and road routes to Berlin. The eleven-month blockade was over. Berlin could breathe again.

The Berlin blockade had one important result. It persuaded the western powers to strengthen their defences against a possible Russian attack. In

April 1949 they formed the North Atlantic Treaty Organisation. Its members were the United States, Canada, Great Britain, France, Denmark, Norway, Iceland, Portugal, Holland, Belgium and Luxembourg. Each of the member states promised to come to the aid of the others if they were attacked by a foreign power.

Communism in China

Just as the Berlin blockade was coming to an end, the western powers began to worry about events in China. For some time a communist revolution had been brewing there. In the summer of 1949 the communist forces, led by Mao Tse-Tung, finally overthrew the government of Chiang Kai-Shek. On 1 October 1949 Mao became chairman of the People's Republic of China. The United States had always supported Chiang Kai-Shek. They therefore saw Mao's victory as another example of the spread of communism. They believed that it made Stalin and communist Russia more powerful than before. This only made them more determined to stop communism spreading any further. Soon they saw a chance of doing this.

The Korean War

In 1945 Japan had been forced to surrender her rule over Korea. Korea had been divided into two separate countries. In North Korea a communist government was established under the control of Stalin. South Korea set up a republic under the leadership of Syngman Rhee.

In June 1950 North Korean armies invaded South Korea in an attempt to bring the whole of Korea under communist control. The western powers

Chiang Kai-Shek, ruler of China 1928–48. After his overthrow Chiang fled to the island Taiwan (Formosa) where he established a government which claimed authority over the whole of China.

Mao Tse-Tung, leader of the People's Republic of China. Born in 1893, the son of a peasant, Mao helped to form the Chinese Communist Party in 1921. He soon came into conflict with the government of Chiang Kai-Shek and civil war broke out in 1927. Although Mao supported Chiang Kai-Shek in fighting against the Japanese during the Second World War, he continued the civil war after Japan's defeat, and finally gained victory in 1949. Since then, as Chairman of the Chinese Communist Party, he has put through many reforms to transform China into a communist state.

275

Syngman Rhee (1875–1965), President of South Korea from 1948 to 1960.

Opposite (top)
Nikita Khruschev (1894–1971), became first secretary of the Russian Communist Party from 1953 to 64 and President of the Council of Ministers from 1958 to 64. He fell from power in 1964, largely because of failures in his agricultural policy. He was always a controversial figure and on one occasion, at a meeting of the United Nations, he took off his shoe and banged it on a table in order to interrupt a speech by the British Prime Minister, Harold Macmillan.

immediately decided that Stalin had encouraged the North Koreans to attack. They believed that it was part of his plan to increase the power of communism in the world. Therefore the United States appealed to the United Nations to intervene in the war on the side of South Korea. The United Nations immediately agreed to send troops. Many of these troops were in fact American, led by General MacArthur. They managed to repel the North Korean invasion. Finally after three years of bitter fighting, an armistice was signed in July 1953. This left the boundaries of North Korea and South Korea roughly where they had been before the beginning of the war.

The Korean War had two important results. In the first place the United States increased the size of her armed forces in order to be ready for any further wars. The American army was trebled in size, and the navy and air force were doubled. In the second place, the people in western Europe became even more afraid that Russia might invade them. They feared a 'European Korea'. Therefore they took steps to strengthen NATO.

The End of the Cold War
During the 1950s the cold war at last began to thaw. In 1953 Stalin died from a sudden heart attack. He was eventually succeeded by Nikita Khruschev, the son of a peasant from the Ukraine. Khruschev had risen to the top through hard work and had been a close favourite of Stalin. However, when Stalin was dead Khruschev began to criticise him. He claimed that Stalin had been a dictator and that he had brought misery to the Russian people.

Khruschev therefore set out to make life more pleasant in Russia. He tried to increase the standard of living by producing more luxury goods such as television sets and motor cars. He once said, 'You cannot put theory in your soup or Marxism into your clothes. If after forty years of communism, a person cannot have a glass of milk or a pair of shoes, he will not believe that communism is a good thing, no matter what you tell him'.

In foreign policy Khruschev adopted a policy of peaceful co-existence. By this he meant that Russia and the United States should live at peace with one another. He realised that the two countries would never agree on many matters. However, he hoped that they could learn to settle their disputes by argument rather than by war. In this way the world would avoid the disaster of a Third World War.

The Hydrogen Bomb
Another event also helped to thaw the cold war. In 1952 the United States exploded the first hydrogen bomb. In 1956 Russia also exploded one. The hydrogen bomb was much more powerful than the atomic bomb and many

times more destructive. Everybody realised that if they were ever used in a 'nuclear war' then they would destroy the whole of Europe's civilisation. Therefore the leaders of the United States and Russia began to avoid the danger of a war with each other. Nowadays, in the 1970s, it does not seem likely that there will be a war between the United States and Russia. The cold war is almost over.

2 The Age of Affluence

Many of the wars that have taken place in Europe since 1760 have been caused by rivalry between different nations. Since 1945 much of the rivalry has disappeared. Nations have now learnt to co-operate with each other. The result has been a period of peace and prosperity.

The Marshall Plan

This co-operation began shortly after the Second World War. The winter of 1946–47 was extremely cold. There were heavy falls of snow and sharp frost all over Europe. This brought industry to a standstill and caused a shortage of food and fuel. Many people were cold and hungry. It seemed as if Europe was on the verge of a complete economic crisis.

However, in June 1947 the American Secretary of State, George C. Marshall, put forward a plan for giving economic aid to Europe. His plan was called the Marshall Plan. By this the United States offered to give large sums of money to Europe provided the separate countries co-operated with one another to decide how it should be spent. Russia refused to take part in the scheme and she prevented the communist countries in eastern Europe from doing so. However, most countries in western Europe did take part. In April 1948 they set up a special organisation, the Organisation for European Economic Co-operation (O.E.E.C.). This decided how to share out the American aid. Between 1948–51 the O.E.E.C. distributed over twelve thousand million dollars. This helped to rebuild the European economy.

The Council of Europe

While the Marshall Plan was being put into effect, several European countries began to work together in other ways. In 1949 the Council of Europe was established. This was a sort of international parliament which contained Great Britain, France, Italy, Ireland, the Netherlands, Belgium, Luxembourg, Denmark, Norway and Sweden. It had no power to make laws or vote taxes. However, it was a useful meeting place where governments could discuss international problems.

George C Marshall (1880–1959), American Secretary of State 1947–8 and author of the Marshall Plan for economic help to Europe.

The E.C.S.C.

In 1950 two Frenchmen suggested a plan for economic co-operation in Europe. Their names were Pierre Monnet and Robert Schuman. They suggested that an international commission should be established to control the production of coal and steel in the various countries of Europe. In this way countries would learn to co-operate with each other in economic matters. After many meetings and discussions the European Coal and Steel Community (E.C.S.C.) was set up in March 1951. Six countries took part in it: France, West Germany, Italy, Belgium, Holland and Luxembourg. They came to be known as the Six.

The Common Market

The E.C.S.C. was a great success. In the first three years the steel production of the participating countries rose by twenty-five per cent. The Six therefore decided to press on with plans for closer economic co-operation. In 1957 they signed the Treaty of Rome. This established the European Economic Community (E.E.C.), which is often called the Common Market. The countries of the Common Market agreed to abolish all tariffs and duties on trade between themselves within fifteen years and to impose a common tariff on imports from outside. They also planned to have common policies on agriculture, transport, wages and prices. In this way they linked up their separate countries into one large economic unit containing over one hundred and eighty million people. This gave them the chance to compete on equal terms with economic giants like the United States and Russia.

Britain and EFTA

When the negotiations for the E.E.C. were taking place, Britain was given the chance to join. She refused, largely because she did not want to lose control over her own economic affairs. Instead she negotiated a trading agreement with six other countries: Austria, Denmark, Portugal, Sweden, Switzerland and Norway. This agreement established the European Free Trade Association (EFTA). EFTA was not as ambitious as the Common Market. The participating countries merely abolished all the tariffs and duties for closer economic co-operation on things such as agriculture and transport.

Britain joins the Common Market

By the early 1960s most people could see that the Common Market was much more successful than EFTA. The industry and trade of the Six was growing more quickly than ever before. Britain therefore changed her mind about the Common Market and made an application to join it. This applica-

Robert Schuman (1886–1963), French Foreign Minister 1947–51, who helped to bring about the formation of the European Coal and Steel Community in 1951. This marked the beginning of political and economic co-operation among the countries of western Europe that led to the establishment of the EEC in 1957.

Member countries of the E.E.C. are shaded on this map.

tion was turned down in 1963, largely because of the attitude of the French President, General de Gaulle. He believed that Britain had too many links with the United States and that she would not co-operate fully in Europe. He also feared that Britain would be a strong rival to France in the Common Market. In 1967 de Gaulle also turned down another British application for membership.

However, in 1969 de Gaulle resigned from office. Britain once again applied for membership, and this time she was successful. In January 1973 she 'went into Europe'. Denmark and Ireland did so too. As a result, the Common Market contained all the major powers of western Europe.

Europe today

By 1970 Europe's importance in the world was slowly declining. The United States and Russia were the world's new 'super-powers', with huge armies and atomic weapons. In the Far East China was also becoming a world power. In the 1960s she exploded her first hydrogen bomb and in 1971 she became a member of the United Nations. In Asia and Africa new nations had been created which demanded a say in world affairs.

This meant that Europe was no longer the most powerful continent in the world. On the contrary, she was badly divided. In eastern Europe most countries were controlled by Russia. In western Europe most countries were friendly with the United States and members of the Common Market.

Nevertheless Europe as a whole was growing steadily more prosperous. People lived in better houses than ever before and they wore better clothes. Many people could afford to own a motor car and household gadgets such as televisions, refrigerators and washing machines. Teenagers could buy 'pop' records and dress in the latest fashions. Children were better educated and more healthy. As a result of this, life became more enjoyable for most people. However, there were still many poor people, especially among the old, the sick and the disabled. There were still terrible slum areas in many cities and towns. There was also discrimination against people because of their political and religious beliefs. All these problems have still to be solved. It is up to ourselves—and to future generations—to solve them.

TO DO

1 You are in Berlin during the blockade of 1948–49. Write an account of your experiences.
2 Try to find out more about Mao Tse-Tung. In what ways has he changed life in China since he came to power in 1949?
3 Try to find out more about the life of Nikita Khruschev.
4 Draw up a list of the advantages and disadvantages of the Common Market.
5 What do you think are the most urgent problems facing the world today?
6 Try to find out more about the way in which clothing fashions have changed since 1945.
7 How has people's taste in popular music changed since 1948?
8 Draw up a list of the ten most important people in the twentieth century. Give reasons for your choice.

TO READ

Modern China, Modern Times, John Robottom, Longman Group.
Western Europe after Hitler, Modern Times, B. J. Elliott, Longman Group.
Modern Russia, Modern Times, John Robottom, Longman Group.
Europe, Making the Modern World, John Robottom (ed.), Longman Group.
Asia, Making the Modern World, John Robottom (ed.), Longman Group.
Russia, Making the Modern World, John Robottom (ed), Longman Group.
America, Making the Modern World, John Robottom (ed.), Longman Group.
Africa and the Middle East, Making the Modern World, John Robottom (ed.), Longman Group.
The Motor Industry, Jackdaw Series no. 77, Jackdaw Publications.
Men and Towns, Jackdaw Series no. 80, Jackdaw Publications.

DATELINE

1947   The Marshall Plan.
1948   April: organisation of the O.E.E.C.
      June: beginning of the Berlin blockade.
1949   Establishment of the Council of Europe.
      October: communist revolution in China.
1950   Beginning of the Korean War.
1951   March: establishment of the E.C.S.C.
1952   U.S.A. explodes the first hydrogen bomb.
1953   March: the death of Stalin.
      July: end of the Korean War.
1957   Treaty of Rome: establishment of the E.E.C. (Common Market).
1973   Britain, Denmark and Ireland join the Common Market.

Glossary

Anti-semitism: Hatred of the Jews.

Armistice: An agreement to end the fighting in a war.

Capitalist: A person who owns land, property or factories.

Communism: The belief that people should sacrifice their property and labour to the community. The idea was made popular by the writings of Karl Marx.

Conservative: A person who opposes change.

Constitution: A set of laws that lays down how a state should be governed.

Democracy: A belief that all adult people should have a say in the government of their country.

Dictator: A ruler who has complete power in a country.

Fascism: The political ideas of Benito Mussolini.

Imperialism: The conquest of foreign territory.

Jacobins: Members of the Jacobin Club in Paris during the French Revolution. They wanted France to become a democratic country.

Legislature: An elected parliament which makes laws for a state.

Proletariat: A term often used to describe the working class.

Radicalism: The belief in the need for drastic political and social reforms.

Sans-culottes: The poor people in France during the French Revolution.

Socialism: The belief that people should sacrifice their own interests and work for the good of the community. Socialism became popular during the nineteenth century through the ideas of Karl Marx.

Soviets: Councils of workers and soldiers who helped to bring about the Russian Revolution of 1917.

Universal Suffrage: The right of every adult person to have a vote.

Veto: The right to reject legislation.

Bibliography

This is a brief guide to further reading on the topics covered in this book. It is intended mainly for teachers but may also be useful for advanced students. As far as possible I have confined the list to paperbacks that are currently in print.

General Textbooks
Palmer A.W. *A Dictionary of Modern History* Penguin 1964
Sellman R.R. *A Historical Atlas* Arnold 2nd edition 1971
Thomas D. *Europe Since Napoleon* Penguin 1966
Wood A. *Europe 1815-1945* Longman Group 1964

Part 1   Europe 1760–1870

Basic Texts
Collins I. *The Age of Progress* Arnold 1964
Droz J. *Europe Between Revolutions 1815-1848* Fontana 1967
Hobsbam E. *Age of Revolution 1789-1845* Mentor 1962
Rudé G. *Revolutionary Europe 1783-1815* Fontana 1964

Change Comes to Europe
Behrens C.B.A. *The Ancien Regime* Thames and Hudson 1967
Hampson N. *The Enlightenment* Penguin 1968
Morris H.B. *The American Revolution: a short history* Anvil Books 1952
Richardson P. *Empire and Slavery* Longman Group 1968

French Revolution
Lefebvre G. *The Coming of the French Revolution* Vintage Books 1947
Rudé G. *Interpretations of the French Revolution* Historical Association Pamphlet 1961
Sydenham M.J. *The French Revolution* University Paperbacks 1965

Napoleon
Holtman R.B. *The Napoleonic Revolution* Lippencott 1967
Markham F. *Napoleon* Weidenfeld and Nicolson 1963

Unification of Italy and Germany
Albrecht-Carrié R. *A Diplomatic History of Europe Since the Congress of Vienna* University Paperbacks 2nd edition 1965

Mack Smith D. *The Making of Italy 1796–1866* Macmillan 1968
Medlicott W.N. *Bismarck and Germany* English University Press 1965
Ramm Agatha *The Risorgimento* Historical Association Pamphlet 1962
Taylor A.J.P. *Bismarck* Mentor 1968

Changes in the Economy
Addy J. *The Agrarian Revolution* Longman Group 1972
Armengaud A. *Population in Europe 1700–1914* Fontana 1970
Cipolla C. *Economic History of World Population* Penguin 1970
Duckham B.F. *The Transport Revolution 1750–1830* Historical Association Pamphlet 1966
Hartwell R.M. *The Industrial Revolution in England* Historical Association Pamphlet 1966
Henderson W.O. *The Industrialisation of Europe 1789–1914* Thames and Hudson 1969
Landes D.S. *Unbound Prometheus. Technical Change and Industrial Development in Western Europe from 1750 to the Present* Cambridge University Press 1969
Moyse-Bartlett *From Sail to Steam* Historical Association Pamphlet 1946

The Social Problem
Collins I. *Liberalism in Nineteenth-Century Europe* Historical Association Pamphlet 1957
Henriques U. *The Early Factory Acts and Their Enforcement* Historical Association Pamphlet 1971
Hunt R.N.C. *The Theory and Practice of Communism* Penguin 1969
Mather F.C. *Chartism* Historical Association Pamphlet 1965
Midwinter E. *Victorian Social Reform* Longman Group 1968
Taylor G. *The Problem of Poverty 1660–1834* Longman Group 1969

Part 2   Europe 1870–1945

Basic Texts
Isaac M.R. *A History of Europe since 1870* Arnold 2nd edition 1971
Roberts J. *Europe 1880–1945* Longman Group 1967
Thompson D. *World History from 1914–1961* Oxford University Press 1963

The Age of Prosperity and Power
Gollwitzer H. *Europe in the Age of Imperialism 1880–1915* Thames and Hudson 1969
Hannah A.J. *European Rule in Africa* Historical Association Pamphlet 1965
Morrell W.P. *The Great Powers in the Pacific* Historical Association Pamphlet 1963

Oliver R. and Fage D.J. *A Short History of Africa* Penguin 1962

First World War
Nicholson H. *Peacemaking 1919* Methuen 1964
Schmitt B. *Origins of the First World War* Historical Association Pamphlet
    1968
Taylor A.J.P. *The First World War: an Illustrated History* Penguin 1970
Turner L.C.F. *The First World War* Warne 1968

Inter-War Years
Bullock A. *Hitler: A Study in Tyranny* Penguin 1969
Carmichael J. *A Short History of the Russian Revolution* London 1966
Deutscher I. *Stalin* Penguin 1970
Hoetzch Otto *The Evolution of Russia* Thames and Hudson 1966
Nettl J. P. *The Soviet Achievement* Thames and Hudson 1967
Smith D. *Left and Right in Twentieth Century Europe* Longman Group 1970
Taylor A.J.P. *From Sarajevo to Potsdam* Thames and Hudson 1966
Wiskemann E. *Europe of the Dictators 1919-1945* Fontana 1970

Second World War
Brown H. *The Second World War* Faber 1968
Medlicott W.N. *The Coming of War in 1939* Historical Association Pamphlet
    1963
Robertson E.M.(ed.) *The Origins of the Second World War* Macmillan 1971

Europe Since 1945
Crouzet M. *The European Renaissance since 1945* Thames and Hudson 1970
Purcell V. *The Rise of Modern China* Historical Association Pamphlet 1962
Schram S. *Mao Tse-Tung* Penguin 1966

Index